Who's Your Mama,
Are You Catholic,
and
Can You Make A Roux?

Book 2

Who's Your Mama,
Are You Catholic,
and
Can You Make A Roux?

Book 2

Marcelle Bienvenu

Acadian House
PUBLISHING
Lafayette, Louisiana

ON THE COVER: *Easter Sunday 1951 found my brother, Henri Clay, and I all dressed up and posing for a picture after Mass. Getting decked out for special occasions – or just for the fun of it – is one of my many fond memories of growing up in south Louisiana in the 1950s and '60s.*

ISBN-13: 978-0-9995884-6-8
ISBN-10: 0-9995884-6-X

♦ **Published by Acadian House Publishing, Lafayette, Louisiana**
  (Edited by Trent Angers; designed and produced by Jon Russo)

To my nieces and nephews and their children,

who are now making new memories

and carrying on our family traditions

and, hopefully, making new ones.

INTRODUCTION

A second helping
of *Who's Your Mama…?*

When I wrote *Who's Your Mama, Are You Catholic, And Can You Make A Roux? (Book 1)* in the late 1980s, I hoped it would be welcomed by the local community, and it was. The title was catchy, and everyone who bought the book seemed to feel a kinship to the stories that accompanied the recipes.

It warmed my heart to read comments like, "The book made me remember our family's gatherings" or "I can relate to the incidents in the book" and "The recipes are for the kind of food I grew up with." Memories are what make our lives rich and full.

Little did I think the book would find its way all over the United States and, yes, to foreign countries. Local folks sent copies of the book to relatives and friends whom they felt would enjoy it.

LOUISIANA

Cajun Country
(Acadiana)

I remember getting a letter from a young man stationed overseas in which he explained that he kept the book by his bed and read a little of it each night before going to sleep. It kept him from getting homesick! College students have told me that when they went off to school their parents tucked a copy of the book in their trunks. Older people tell me they value their copies because the book reminds them of "the good times."

For years I received requests to write another book. This second book was published originally in 1998 but went out of print in 2003. But there was still lots of demand for it, so here it is again.

It's much like the first book, but with different stories and new recipes, of course. The recipes are not fancy, because that's not our style here in south Louisiana. We like good food made with simple ingredients that are readily at hand.

Like the first book, this one features stories related to food because food is such an important part of my family's life and traditions. Since the original publication of Book 1 (1989), my family has grown a lot – and is still growing – so new traditions and recipes are being introduced and added to our repertoire.

I hope you will enjoy reading this book as much as I enjoyed writing it.

– Marcelle Bienvenu

TABLE OF CONTENTS

ACKNOWLEDGEMENTS

I would like to thank a number of people who, in one way or another, helped to make this book a reality:

My husband Rock Lasserre who is always supportive and encouraging.

My brothers Henri Clay and Bruce Bienvenu and my sister Edna and their respective spouses who sustain our family's heritage and traditions.

My editor and publisher, Trent Angers, who agreed to republish this book; and Jon Russo for his patience and dedication in producing this new edition.

Who's Your Mama,

Are You Catholic,

and
Can You Make A Roux ?

Book 2

Enjoying ourselves at a Mardi Gras party some time in the 1970s are, left to right, my Mama, Rhena Judice Bienvenu; my sister, Edna; and me. So much of what I know about Louisiana cooking I learned from Mama.

SPRING

Although winters in Louisiana are drab, dull and gray, spring is a showcase of color.

After the last cold days of February, March blows in wet and windy.

April breezes in with splashes of color. Bright pink and purple azaleas, stark white bridal wreath, radiant redbud, and creamy, snow-white wild dogwood burst out in brilliance against the pale green new leaves budding on the bald cypress and graceful live oaks. Lush green clover bobs along the highways and byways, and giant wild elephant ears rise along the banks of languid bayous and streams.

It is the time of year that I take stock of our great state. In the northern half of the state that begins around Alexandria, the terrain is dry and hilly. We may not often realize that the waters of half a continent churn south through Louisiana in the formidable currents of the Mississippi River and its tributary, the Red River.

In Louisiana's delta region, where the Mississippi and its main distributary, the Atchafalaya, meander to the Gulf of Mexico, the land is mostly flat and wet with freshwater swamps and open salt marshes alive with a plethora of our favorite seafood.

Crawfish season, which runs loosely from January to June, is in full swing, and when the snow in the North begins to melt the rivers in the South swell. Fishermen head to bays, rivers and the open waters of the Gulf. Ah, there will be a bounty of crabs, shrimp and fish to prepare for meals taken in the cool of the evening.

It's time to get out of the house, enjoy the great outdoors, and, of course, indulge in good food.

Crawfish galore

At the height of crawfish season, signs in front of seafood markets and grocery stores and alongside crawfish farms appear hawking the crustacean crop. The crawfish price war is on!

One afternoon I observed prices ranging from $6.99 to $4.99 for a pound of peeled crawfish tails. Here in south Louisiana, everyone wants a bargain, but one has to be skeptical and read the packages carefully. Some packers put only 12 ounces per bag, thus the price appears to be lower, but mostly the crawfish tails are sold by the pound. I must tell you that I buy only Louisiana crawfish – none of that imported crawfish for me.

After some comparative shopping, I usually find my bargain, and that's when I spring for several packages of peeled and about 40 pounds of live crawfish to boil for my very own crawfish festival.

Oh, in case you don't know, every year there's a huge crawfish festival in the quaint little town of Breaux Bridge that honors Monsieur Crawfish. For three days, throngs of visitors join the locals for contests ranging from crawfish eating to crawfish cooking. There's plenty of dancing, partying and general frivolity.

Most of the time I like to celebrate those wonderful freshwater crustaceans in the peace and quiet of my tree-shaded back yard on the banks of Bayou Teche with a few close friends.

My husband Rock and I go through the same ritual year after year when we hold our annual crawfish feast.

An old cypress table is dusted off and covered with newspapers on which will be spread heaps of just-boiled, well-seasoned crawfish, potatoes and corn on the cob.

And if that isn't enough, I usually have a pot of crawfish *etouffee*, perhaps some crawfish corn bread, and, at times, this gumbo made with smothered okra prepared during the summer and frozen for just such an occasion.

Crawfish-Okra Gumbo

Makes 6 to 8 servings

1 stick (8 tablespoons) of butter
1 cup of chopped yellow onions
½ cup of chopped bell peppers
1 (16-ounce) can of whole tomatoes, chopped, with their liquid
½ cup of medium-brown roux
4 cups of chicken or shrimp stock
2 pounds of peeled crawfish tails
3 cups of smothered okra (page 36)
Salt and cayenne, to taste

Heat the butter over medium heat in a large, heavy pot or Dutch oven.

Add the onions and bell peppers, and cook, stirring, until they are soft and lightly golden, 8 to 10 minutes. Add the tomatoes and cook, stirring occasionally, for 10 minutes longer.

Add the roux and blend well. Add the chicken or shrimp stock and bring to a gently boil. Cook, stirring occasionally, for 30 minutes.

Add the crawfish tails and the okra, season with salt and cayenne, reduce the heat to medium-low and simmer for 10 minutes more.

Serve with steamed white rice.

Fried Crawfish Tails

Makes 4 appetizer servings

Vegetable oil for deep frying
1 pound of peeled crawfish tails
Salt and cayenne, to taste
1 large egg
Dash of distilled white vinegar
¼ cup of water
1 teaspoon of baking powder
¼ cup of all-purpose flour
¼ cup of Italian-style bread crumbs

Heat the oil to 360 degrees in a deep, heavy pot or electric fryer.

Season the crawfish with salt and cayenne.

In a small bowl, beat the egg and add the vinegar, water and baking powder, and mix well. Add the crawfish tails.

In another bowl, combine the flour and bread crumbs, and season with salt and cayenne.

Drain the crawfish tails, and then toss them in the flour and bread crumb mixture. Shake off excess.

Drop the tails, a few at a time, into the hot oil and fry until golden brown. Drain on paper towels.

Serve hot with tartar sauce.

Creole Tartar Sauce

Makes about 1½ cups

1 cup of mayonnaise
1 tablespoon of Creole mustard
1 teaspoon of Worcestershire sauce
1 teaspoon of fresh lemon juice
1/2 teaspoon of minced garlic
1 tablespoon of sweet pickle relish
2 teaspoons of chopped fresh parsley leaves
1 tablespoon of finely chopped green onions
  (green part only)
1/8 teaspoon of Tabasco
Freshly ground black pepper, to taste

Combine all of the ingredients in a mixing bowl and stir to mix. Cover and chill for at least an hour before serving.

Seafood suppers, outdoors

Years ago, what was known in our family circle as Mama's "back patio" was the hub of our outdoor dining in spring and summer. Practically every evening found us, a few friends, and a neighbor or two gathered together for a seafood supper.

Coleman lanterns were hung on the low, sweeping branches of an oak tree, and Papa was in his glory cooking most of the meal over a fire built in a custom-made iron grate that was his pride and joy.

Those were the days when we boiled dozens of crabs and pounds of shrimp and crawfish. There was always fresh fish – baked, fried or simmered in a *bouillabaisse.*

Very often there was plenty of food left over, but be assured, nothing went to waste. The boiled crabs were picked for the crabmeat to use for crab chops, stew or salad. Shrimp was coarsely chopped and made into shrimp burgers.

Mama and I were reliving those wonderful times not too very long ago while we sat on the patio sipping our gin and tonics with a squeeze of lime. The big oak tree toppled during a hurricane several years ago, and Papa's grate is now nothing more than a pile of rusted metal, but the memories are still quite fresh in our minds.

We had an idea. Why not treat ourselves to our own small bash? Mama admitted to having a couple of pounds of fresh shrimp to make a salad. I went off in search of lump crabmeat to make this appetizer.

My father, Blackie Bienvenu, holds me at my christening in March of 1945. He was a newspaperman who owned and ran The Teche News in St. Martinville, which was later taken over by my brother, Henri Clay. My interest in journalism was born in the 1950s, when I helped my father at the newspaper.

Crabmeat Amandine

Makes 4 appetizer servings

6 tablespoons of butter, melted
1 pound of lump crabmeat, picked over for
   shells and cartilage
1 teaspoon of fresh lemon juice
½ cup of finely chopped green onions
½ cup of toasted almond slivers
Salt and cayenne, to taste
Toast points

Heat the butter in a large skillet over low heat. Add the crabmeat, lemon juice, green onions and almonds. Toss gently. Season with salt and cayenne.

Cook for two minutes, and serve with toast points.

Allow me another seafood memory.

One late spring day found me cruising along La. Hwy. 1, which runs alongside Bayou Lafourche from Donaldsonville to the Gulf of Mexico. Bayou Lafourche has often been called "the longest main street in the world," and it is said that news travels quickly as fishermen, trappers and neighbors pass the word along as they putt-putt down the waterway.

Along the bayou banks just about everyone has a home garden and hand-made signs, tacked on trees and garage posts, advertising "cukes, 'zucs and 'matoes" when the harvest is abundant.

The hardy Acadians who make their homes along this bayou live by land and sea. Their summer gardens, bountiful with cucumbers, zucchini, tomatoes, peppers and corn, along with shrimp, crabs and fish caught in the Gulf, supply their tables with the freshest foods from earth and water.

Having a weakness for garden vegetables, I made several stops before I reached my destination in Galliano, where I was to board an old oyster cutter for a cruise along the bayou to what the locals call Fouchon, a place where the calm bayou joins the choppy waters of the Gulf of Mexico.

While our captain let out the anchor, we watched a steady flow of traffic as ocean-going tugs, oilfield workboats and graceful Lafitte skiffs equipped with shrimp nets made their way out to the open waters.

We settled in for a day in the sun. Children paddled the dingy to the rocky jetties while some adults opted for an excursion in a small sailboat that we brought along. Others chose to join the dolphins that came to play in the water near our boat.

When the sun began to fall in the western sky, we took up anchor and followed the shrimp boats back up the bayou. Noisy seagulls, looking for a bit of supper from the discards of the shrimp boats, joined the parade.

It was dusk when we docked. While people gathered up their ice chests, bathing suits and other paraphernalia, I bargained with a shrimper who was sorting out his catch. He parted with a couple of pounds of shrimp and a dozen crabs. With my vegetable cache and my food from the sea, the next night's supper was a done deal.

*My brother, Henri Clay, and I pose for our annual Easter season
picture in 1947.*

Shrimp & Crab Lafourche

Makes about 8 servings

2 pounds of medium-size shrimp, headed, peeled, and deveined (reserve heads and shells)
2 tablespoons of butter
1 tablespoon of olive oil
1 cup of chopped yellow onions
4 ears of fresh corn, shucked and cleaned
3 medium-size ripe tomatoes, peeled, seeded, and chopped
2 cups of shrimp stock
1 pound of lump crabmeat, picked over for shells and cartilage
¼ teaspoon of dried basil
Salt and cayenne, to taste

Place the shrimp heads and shells in a stockpot, add enough water to cover, and bring to a boil. Reduce the heat and simmer for 30 minutes.

Drain and reserve the stock. Set aside.

In a large skillet, heat the butter and olive oil over medium heat.

Add the onions and cook, stirring, until soft, three to four minutes.

Add the shrimp and cook until they turn pink, about three to four minutes.

Cut the corn off the cob and press out the milk from the cob with a knife. Add the corn and the tomatoes to the pot and cook for five minutes, stirring occasionally.

Add two cups of shrimp stock and the lump crabmeat. Simmer gently for three minutes. Season with the basil, salt and cayenne.

Serve in deep bowls over hot rice.

This dish left me hungry for more crabs. The seafood market, just a few miles from my house, usually has some of the best lump crabmeat, and this is just one of the ways I like to enjoy fresh crabmeat.

Artichoke Bottoms with Lump Crabmeat

Makes 10 appetizer servings

3 pounds of lump crabmeat, picked over for shells and cartilage
2 cups of mayonnaise
½ cup of chopped green onions (green part only)
2 tablespoons of capers, drained
¼ teaspoon of chopped dill
Salt and freshly ground black pepper, to taste
10 large artichoke bottoms
Toast points
Tomato wedges

Toss the crabmeat with the mayonnaise, onions, capers and dill. Season with salt and pepper.

Spoon equal portions of the crabmeat onto the artichoke bottoms. This dish may be warmed in a 250-degree oven for 10 minutes or served slightly chilled.

To serve, surround the artichoke bottoms with toast points and a garnish of tomato wedges dusted with your favorite Creole seasoning.

Brussels sprouts are not grown locally but are available at the markets throughout the winter and early spring. My husband Rock loves them, especially when they are prepared in the following manner. Oh, and he says they make a nice accompaniment to bright red tomatoes.

Rock's Brussels Sprouts

Makes 4 servings

1 pound of fresh brussels sprouts,
   trimmed at the base
4 cups of water
¼ teaspoon of salt
3 tablespoons of sour cream
Pinch of grated nutmeg
1 teaspoon of Creole mustard
1 teaspoon of chopped fresh parsley leaves
Freshly ground black pepper, to taste

Rinse the sprouts under cool water.

Combine the water and salt in a medium-size saucepan over medium-high heat and bring to a boil. Add the sprouts, reduce the heat to medium-low, cover, and cook for three to four minutes.

Remove from the heat and let stand, covered, for three to four minutes longer, or until the sprouts are just tender. Drain.

In a medium-size mixing bowl, combine the sour cream, nutmeg, mustard and parsley and stir to blend. Add the sprouts and toss gently to coat evenly.

Season with the black pepper and serve warm.

Rock also adores sweet onions. Down here in the South, Vidalias from Georgia appear in our markets during the spring, and we can't seem to get enough of them. We make onion pie and onion soup, or serve them thinly sliced with tomatoes and cucumbers, and sometimes we roast them like this. Use any of the varieties of sweet onions available in your area.

Roasted Vidalia Onions

Makes 4 servings

4 medium-size Vidalia onions
5 tablespoons of olive oil
2 tablespoons of red wine vinegar
1 teaspoon of Creole or Dijon mustard
Salt and freshly ground black pepper, to taste

Preheat the oven to 400 degrees.

Rub the skin of the onions with two tablespoons of the oil and place them in a pie pan. Bake for about an hour or until soft to the touch. Remove from the oven and let cool.

With a sharp knife, split open the skin, pop out the flesh, and either slice or quarter the onions.

In a medium-size mixing bowl, combine the remaining three tablespoons of oil, the vinegar and mustard. Whisk to blend, add the onions, and season with salt and pepper. Combine the mixture with the onions and toss to blend.

Serve at room temperature.

On yet another boating excursion one fine spring day, food was the topic of conversation. This proves my theory that just about everyone in south Louisiana has a 24-hour-a-day love affair with food. If we're not cooking it, we are eating it. When we're not eating, we're talking about the next meal.

It was a real jewel of a day. Rock and I joined several couples and we journeyed in several boats down the Vermilion River from Lafayette to a spot below Intracoastal City called Boston (pronounced Bos-tahn by the locals) Canal. We delighted in the scenery of budding

Easter Sunday 1951 found my brother, Henri Clay, and I all dressed up and posing for a picture after Mass. I loved getting dressed up – and still do – but Henri Clay, like other boys in our town, wasn't crazy about the idea.

wild iris, dogwood and azalea, and the bright new green leaves on the willow and cypress trees.

Upon arrival at our destination, our hosts fired up the barbecue pit and we were soon munching on sausage po-boys, potato salad and baked beans. During our return trip we scoffed down chocolate cake and lemon cookies.

As we went through the exercise of pulling up the boats, we talked about supper. Rock wanted grilled redfish. My mouth watered for a nice juicy steak. Chicken stew was the choice of Baby Brother Bruce.

Then out of the blue, Julie, one our boat companions, said she thought "copper pennies" would be great with the stew. I had no idea what she was talking about. She explained:

"You know carrots are not only good for you, they really are versatile. You can boil 'em, eat 'em raw, throw them in salads and they add a depth of flavor to soups and sauces."

"What *are* copper pennies?" I asked quietly.

Everyone stared at me in disbelief. They all rushed to talk at once, explaining how to fix this dish.

Early the next morning Julie arrived with her recipe in hand.

I made the copper pennies and loved them. You can serve these either cold or warm.

Growing up in St. Martinville, practically everyone in our neighborhood had a family pet or two or several. Posing in our back yard around 1952 are, left to right, Lennie Nugier, my brother Henri Clay, Jack Nugier and my sister Edna. That's me squatting in the front.

'Copper Pennies'

Makes 6 to 8 servings

2 pounds of raw carrots, cut crosswise into
   thin slices (like pennies)
1 medium yellow onion, sliced very thin
1 medium green bell pepper, seeded and
   chopped
1 clove of garlic, minced
1 (10¾-ounce) can of tomato soup
½ cup of vegetable oil
½ cup of sugar
½ cup of white distilled vinegar
1 teaspoon of dry mustard
1 tablespoon of Worcestershire sauce
Salt and freshly ground black pepper,
   to taste

Boil the carrots until they are just tender, then drain. Place the carrots in a large casserole dish and cover with the onion, bell pepper and garlic.

In a saucepan, boil the rest of the ingredients.

Pour this sauce over the carrot mixture and refrigerate overnight.

Copper pennies go well, by the way, with Sticky Chicken, also known sometimes as chicken *aux gros onions* (chicken with lots of onions) in our part of the state. The nice thing about this dish is that you can add sweet corn, or young peas and mushrooms, or all three, which makes it one of those one-pot dishes we are so fond of in Louisiana. Serve the stuff over steamed rice, and you've got one heck of a meal.

You can use a fryer, but a young roasting chicken is my choice since you can cook it longer without it falling off the bones, and it has much more flavor.

The Bienvenu siblings celebrate little brother Bruce's birthday in 1957. Left to right are Henri Clay, me, Bruce and Edna.

Sticky Chicken

Makes 4 to 6 servings

1 fryer or roasting chicken, about 3 pounds,
   cut into serving pieces
Salt and cayenne, to taste
3 tablespoons of vegetable oil
4 cups of sliced yellow onions
1 cup of sliced green bell peppers
1 cup of whole-kernel corn (optional)
1 cup of green peas (optional)
1½ cups of sliced fresh white button
   mushrooms (optional)

Season the chicken generously with salt and cayenne.

In a large, heavy pot, heat the oil over medium heat, add the chicken, and brown evenly. Add a cup of water to make a gravy.

Add the onions and, stirring occasionally, cook them for about 8 to 10 minutes. Add the bell peppers and cook until they are wilted, about five minutes, stirring occasionally. Season with salt and cayenne, cover the pot with a lid, and lower the heat.

Cook until the chicken is very tender, about an hour. You might have to add a little water to prevent the chicken from sticking during the cooking time.

About 10 minutes before you want to serve, you may choose to add the corn, peas and mushrooms.

Serve over steamed rice.

Easter time and the Cajun microwave

Easter is always a joyous occasion in our family. Going to church together – the ladies wearing their new spring bonnets and the gentlemen attired in linen or seersucker suits – begins the day. After church we usually enjoy a barbecue dinner in Mama's big tree-shaded yard.

One particular Easter Sunday, just as we returned from church, Uncle A.P. (Adolph Preval), sometimes known as Pete, or occasionally as "Pomp," called to invite us to see the pig he was cooking in his "Cajun microwave."

This Cajun microwave is a box-like affair, about five feet long, three feet wide, 20 inches deep, and sometimes, but not always, mounted on four legs. The inside can be lined with metal, but Pomp does not like the metal lining, claiming that it produces too much heat and makes it difficult to roast the pig at an even temperature. A wood-framed metal lid sits on top to hold the charcoal.

We agreed to make a stop at Pomp and Aunt Git's house on the way to Mama's. Rock likes Pomp's style, and his admiration soared even higher when we pulled into Pomp's back yard. There Pomp sat graciously on an old kitchen chair situated on a flatbed trailer alongside his smoking Cajun microwave, a cold highball in hand.

We were allowed to peek at the 50-some-odd-pound pig slowly roasting in the box. The aroma made me want to pinch off a piece of the bubbling skin, but my hand was quickly pushed away.

"He's not ready yet!" Pomp laughed.

Sitting on stools around the trailer, we munched on Aunt Git's boudin and hogshead cheese while Pomp told us how he had put the pig on at 6:30 that morning and had been babysitting it ever since. He planned to stay close to it until it was done.

Rock was settling in, but I reminded him we were expected at Mama's. We promised to return later for our piece of the pig. As we bounced along the gravel road I told Rock about some of Pomp's antics as a young man.

I recalled how, years ago, he almost crippled himself trying to fly a home-made one-man helicopter through a field, and about Winky, his pet monkey who rode on his shoulder everywhere he went, and about the time Pomp tried to teach several of us how to drive and we went through a closed barn door in my grandfather's prized Army jeep.

Several hours later we returned for some pig. It was perfectly done. The skin was crunchy and brown, the meat tender and perfectly seasoned.

We don't have a Cajun microwave, or otherwise we would have tried our hands at a pig the very next weekend, but we did get our fill of pork by having some stuffed pork chops served with a great rice dish *and* stuffed potatoes. Yes, we do like our starches down here.

*Gathering Easter eggs in my back yard in St. Martinville in 2004
are me and my great-nephew, Shane Bennett.*

Stuffed Pork Chops

Makes 4 servings

4 center-cut pork chops, about 1½ inches
    thick (about 8 ounces each)
1/4 cup of coarsely chopped red onions
4 tablespoons of crumbled Roquefort cheese
1/2 teaspoon of coarsely ground
    black pepper
Olive oil
Salt and cayenne, to taste
1/2 teaspoon of garlic powder
1/3 cup of chicken broth
1/3 cup of water

Preheat oven to 400 degrees.

With a sharp knife, cut a pocket into each pork chop. Place a tablespoon of onion, a tablespoon of the crumbled cheese, and 1/8 teaspoon of black pepper into each pocket of the chops. Rub each chop with olive oil and season with salt, cayenne and garlic powder.

Lay the chops in a lightly oiled roasting pan and place in the hot oven to brown for 10 minutes. Reduce the oven temperature to 350 degrees, add the chicken broth and water, cover the pan, and bake until the juices run clear, about an hour and 15 minutes.

Baste the chops several times with the pan juices during the baking process.

Rice with Caramelized Onions

Makes 4 to 6 servings

¾ cup of finely chopped yellow onions
¼ cup of olive oil
½ teaspoon of sugar
1½ cups of long-grain white rice
1 teaspoon of salt
½ teaspoon of white pepper
1 cup of beef broth
1 cup of water
1 tablespoon of chopped pimiento

In a large, heavy saucepan, cook the onions in the oil with the sugar over medium heat until the onions are golden brown, about five minutes.

Add the rice, salt and white pepper and cook the mixture, stirring until the rice begins to turn a little brown. Add the broth and water and boil the mixture, uncovered, over medium heat for 10 minutes.

Reduce the heat to low and cover the saucepan. Cook for 10 to 15 minutes until the rice is tender.

Add the pimiento, fluff the rice, and let stand for five minutes before serving.

Relaxing in my back yard in St. Martinville on a Sunday afternoon in the spring of 2004 are, left to right, my sister, Edna; my brother, Henri Clay; and Edna's husband, Al Landry.

Stuffed Potatoes

Makes about 6 servings

12 medium-sized red potatoes
2 cups of finely chopped yellow onions
3 tablespoons of minced garlic
¼ pound of tasso or spiced ham,
   finely chopped
Salt, cayenne, and garlic powder, to taste
Vegetable oil

The potatoes may be peeled or un-peeled or the skins may be scored according to your preference. To bore the holes through the centers of the potatoes for stuffing, you can use an apple corer, or you can use the handle of a spoon to scrape out the inside of the potato. Do not scrape the potato too aggressively because you want fairly fine potato pieces to be scraped from the inside of the potato.

Finely chop the potato pieces and mix them with the onions, garlic and tasso. Season the mixture with salt, cayenne and garlic powder. Stuff the potatoes with this mixture.

Cover the bottom of a large black iron pot with the cooking oil. Add the potatoes, making sure that all of the potatoes make contact with the bottom of the pot. Cook over medium heat, covered, until the potatoes are done.

You will usually have some of the stuffing left over. Add this to the pot after the potatoes are slightly brown. Add a small amount of water to "raise the bottom" to make a gravy.

Spaghetti time with my great-niece

One spring I was pressed into baby-sitting duties for my great-niece, Madison, who was then 18 months old, while her mother and father finished up their last semester of college. I really didn't mind since I had a loose schedule and she wasn't much trouble. She liked to *roder*, which means "to roam the roads."

Tucked into her car seat with her bottle in hand, she was happy as a clam while we made our rounds of the post office, the bank, the library and the cleaners. She giggled in delight as we went up and down the aisles at the supermarket.

At my house, she was perfectly contented seated on the floor in front of the CD player. She favored, and still does, Cajun music, Jimmy Buffet (whom she calls Jimmy Muffin), Michael Bolton, and the music from *The Lion King*. But most of all, she loved to eat. Creamy grits, mashed bananas and apples sprinkled with cinnamon were some of her favorites.

But what really made her happy is the same dish that makes me very happy – a bowl of spaghetti.

With napkins tucked under our chins and comfortably seated around the coffee table, we slurped down our lunch. In time, I taught her how to eat in a more ladylike manner, but it sure was fun making a little noise and letting the sauce dribble down our chins. For a time our batches of sauces were quite simple and very mild, but now that she's older she's requesting more sophisticated versions.

About once a week she spends an afternoon with me and we juke around the kitchen to the sounds of old Jimmy Muffin, making all sorts of spaghetti sauces. I think you'll like these!

My husband Rock's grandson, Cameron Lasserre, and my great-niece, Madison Alford, seem to be enjoying themselves while playing in our back yard some time around 1994.

Spaghetti Sauce with Olives

Makes 6 to 8 servings

3 (8-ounce) cans of tomato sauce
1 (8 ounces) can of Italian-style
 tomato paste
1 tablespoon of lemon juice
1 tablespoon of dark brown sugar
1/3 cup of red wine vinegar
1/2 teaspoon of dried oregano leaves
1/2 teaspoon of dried basil leaves
3 tablespoons of grated Romano cheese
2 tablespoons of olive oil
1 pound of lean ground beef
1/2 cup of sliced ripe olives
3/4 cup of chopped onion
1/2 cup of chopped celery
1 tablespoon of chopped garlic
1 cup of sliced fresh mushrooms
Salt, to taste
Red pepper flakes, to taste

In a large saucepan, combine the tomato sauce, tomato paste, lemon juice, sugar, vinegar, oregano, basil and cheese. Bring to a boil, reduce the heat, and simmer for 20 minutes, stirring occasionally.

In a skillet, heat the oil over medium-high heat and brown the beef. Add the olives, onions, celery and garlic and cook until the vegetables are soft, about four to five minutes. Add the mushrooms and cook, stirring occasionally, until they are slightly soft, about two to three minutes.

Add the vegetables to the tomato mixture. Season with the salt and red pepper flakes. Serve over the cooked pasta of your choice.

Spaghetti Sauce with Bacon

Makes 4 servings

3 tablespoons of olive oil
1/3 cup of chopped onions
1 teaspoon of chopped garlic
1 cup of chopped artichoke hearts (canned,
 packed in water)
3 (8-ounce) cans of tomato sauce
1/3 cup of fresh lemon juice
2 tablespoons of chopped parsley
Salt, black pepper, and Tabasco sauce,
 to taste
8 strips of crisply fried bacon, coarsely
 crumbled
Grated Romano cheese

Heat the oil in a large skillet over medium heat. Add the onions, garlic and artichokes. Cook, stirring often, until the onions are golden, about eight minutes.

Add the tomato sauce, lemon juice and parsley. Season with salt, black pepper and Tabasco and bring the sauce to a boil. Reduce the heat and simmer for 15 minutes, stirring occasionally.

Remove from the heat, add the bacon, and serve over cooked pasta sprinkled with Romano cheese.

*Water skiing on Catahoula Lake is one of the many summertime activities
we enjoyed growing up in south Louisiana in the 1950s and '60s. We
also liked swimming, fishing, crabbing and eating watermelon.*

SUMMER

All my life I've enjoyed the summer. When I was young I couldn't wait for school to close, for that meant Mama and Papa were going to take all of us kids, along with a few cousins, to either the camp on Catahoula Lake near the Atchafalaya Basin or to the one at Cypremort Point on Vermilion Bay.

We were wild with excitement when we packed the station wagon with inner tubes, swim suits and bags of groceries. Ah, a week or two away from it all was absolute heaven as far as I was concerned.

It was hot, to be sure, but ceiling fans and breezes blowing from the water brought relief from the heat. At bedtime, Mama sprinkled baby powder on our sheets to keeps us cool during the night.

We fished, we crabbed, we went swimming; we ate ice cold watermelon chilled in big washtubs by the back steps.

Then it was home again, but the summer still stretched before me. Some afternoons I nestled in the hammock in the back yard and read the afternoon away. There were trips to the snowball stand for the best-ever flavored snowballs made with the finest crushed ice you ever put in your mouth. We went water-skiing in the bayou or on the lake, and later, when I was older, we drank ice cold beer while lounging on the piers and wharves that jutted out over the water.

During the summer Mama and Papa entertained almost nightly with fish frys, crab boils and barbecues. We made gallons and gallons of homemade ice cream and lemonade to enjoy on the expansive patio, lush with sweet-smelling gardenias and jasmine, bright red hibiscus, and trailing vines of passion flowers.

Oh, yes, the summers are always magical to me. These days I like nothing better than sitting on a patio in the evening to listen to the crickets and bullfrogs or to watch the fireflies darting around the banana trees and bamboo. Both sunrises and sunsets are spectacular in the summer, and I love to hear the sound of squealing children playing hide-and-seek among the darkening shadows at the end of a hot, steamy day.

It's a time when Rock and I entertain, much like Mama and Papa did years ago, but on our very own patio. We take guests on boat rides up and down Bayou Teche and point out the herons and the wild elephant ears lining the banks. It's a time to enjoy outings at camps and summer cottages with friends and relatives where food is, as usual, the focal point.

I wish summer would never end.

My husband, Rock Lasserre, and I share a loving moment on our wedding anniversary in 1999. We were married on October 6, 1990.

'Putting up' summer vegetables

One of the telltale signs that summer had arrived was when Mama would put aside a day or two to "put up" summer vegetables. She was particularly fond of eggplant, corn and okra, and nothing, I mean nothing, would stand in her way when she was hell-bent on her task.

On one such occasion, she called me to assist in chopping onions, bell peppers and celery for her. We worked like

Trojans for several hours and then took a lunch break. I would have been satisfied with a ham and tomato sandwich, but, no, Mama had put a chicken to roasting. The chicken was superlative, crisp on the outside and moist within. A salad of sliced tomatoes dabbed with her famous homemade mayonnaise and a rice dressing made with eggplant rounded out the meal.

Eggplant & Rice Dressing

Makes 6 servings

1 large eggplant, peeled and diced
2 tablespoons of vegetable oil
1 cup of chopped yellow onions
1/2 cup of chopped green bell peppers
1 pound of lean ground beef
1/4 cup of chicken broth
4 cups of cooked long-grain white rice
1/3 cup of minced fresh parsley leaves
Salt and cayenne, to taste

Put the eggplant in a deep bowl filled with cool, salted water and let stand for about 15 minutes. Drain the eggplant and rinse with fresh, cool water. Pat dry with paper towels.

In a large, heavy pot, heat the oil over medium heat, add the eggplant, and cook until the eggplant begins to soften, about five minutes. Add the onions and bell peppers and cook until the vegetables begin to wilt, two to four minutes.

Add the ground beef, reduce to medium-low and cook for about 30 minutes, until the eggplant is soft and very tender.

Add the chicken broth if the mixture

becomes too dry. Add the rice, mixing well. Add the parsley and season with salt and cayenne.

We continued our work through the afternoon before Mama took off her apron and announced it was quitting time.

Thank you, Lord!

Before I took my leave I helped her label the array of jars to be stashed in the freezer. Just as I walked out of the door, she hugged me and whispered, "Thank you, *chere*." Then she handed me a couple of her prized eggplants and a recipe for eggplant and veal meatballs.

Eggplant & Veal Meatballs

Makes 12 meatballs

2 tablespoons of vegetable oil
1 pound of ground veal
3 tablespoons of olive oil
1 large eggplant, peeled and diced
½ cup of minced yellow onions
3 garlic cloves, minced
2 large eggs
Salt and freshly ground black pepper, to taste
Italian-style bread crumbs
12 thin slices of Muenster cheese

Preheat the oven to 350 degrees.

Heat the vegetable oil in a large, heavy skillet over medium heat. Add the ground veal and cook, stirring, until all the pink has disappeared. Set aside.

In another skillet, heat the olive oil over medium heat, add the eggplant and cook, stirring, until it becomes very tender. Mash it with a fork. Add the onions, garlic and veal, and cook, stirring, for 10 minutes.

Transfer the mixture from the skillet to a mixing bowl and cool for about 10 minutes. Add the eggs, and mix. Season with salt and pepper. Add enough bread crumbs so that the mixture is thick enough to bind into meatballs. Form meatballs, place in a baking pan, and bake for 20 minutes.

Top with slices of cheese and return to oven for five minutes or until the cheese melts.

For years I watched Mama and her aunts go through the ritual of pickling and preserving everything imaginable – mirlitons, figs, okra, watermelon rinds, pears and berries. There used to be an outside kitchen behind Tante May's house used solely for this purpose. There was a long work table where they sat peeling, chopping and cleaning. An old gas stove stood in one corner and a large deep sink occupied another. Once the aunts got their pots and pans going, the tiny room was like a furnace, but the aromas that floated through the screen windows made me yearn for chilly mornings when pear preserves could be piled on breakfast crepes or corn bread.

I still adore the taste of pickled mirlitons and okra, and sometimes I dunk them in my martinis.

The aunts and their kitchen are gone now, but I've taken up the chore of canning and preserving, using, of course, their old recipes.

The pears that we use to make preserves are those grown in Louisiana primarily for this purpose. They are commonly called "canning" pears and are quite firm.

Remember, when canning pears, or anything, for that matter, it's very important to carefully read the directions that come with the canning jars that are specifically designed for preserving and canning.

Pear Preserves

Makes about 2 pints

6 cups of peeled, cored, and sliced pears
2 cups of granulated sugar

Put the pears in a large bowl and cover with cold water. Let stand for one hour.

Drain off the water, put the pears in a plastic container, and cover with the sugar. Let stand overnight. By the next day, there should be a lot of syrup in the container.

Pour the pears with the sugar and the syrup into a nonreactive pot and cook over medium-low heat, stirring occasionally to prevent sticking, for about three hours, or until the mixture thickens and the pears are translucent and tender.

Pour equal amounts of the mixture into sterilized pint-size jars. Then process the jars in a hot water bath for 15 minutes.

Cool and store in a dark, cool place.

Honey Pears

Makes 5 half-pints

3 pounds of firm pears
2 quarts of water
2 teaspoons of salt
5 cups of sugar

Peel and core the pears. Combine the water and salt, pour over the pears, and soak for one hour. Drain and grind the pears in a food processor.

Measure out eight cups of the ground pears and combine with the sugar in a large pot. Cook pears and sugar slowly for 1½ to 2 hours, stirring often, until the mixture is golden brown.

Pour into hot, sterilized jars and seal.

Pickled Okra

Makes 5 pints

2 pounds of young okra pods (Select small
    ones, 2 to 3 inches long.)
2½ teaspoons of celery seeds
2½ teaspoons of crushed dried red pepper
2½ teaspoons of mustard seeds
15 cloves of garlic

VINEGAR MIXTURE
4 cups of distilled white vinegar
2 cups of water
½ cup of salt

Rinse the okra in cool water and pat dry. Soak in ice water for an hour. Drain and pat the okra dry again and place them upside down in sterilized pint jars.

Into each jar put one-half teaspoon of celery seed, one-half teaspoon of red pepper, one-half teaspoon of mustard seed, and three cloves of garlic.

Bring the vinegar mixture to a boil and pour it in the jars, completely covering the okra. Seal the jars tightly. Process in a hot water bath for 10 minutes.

Allow the pickled okra to age for several weeks before using. The okra is best when it is chilled before serving.

Mama poses with my sister Edna and her son Nicholas, in 1987.

'Smothering' okra

While I'm on the subject of okra, I must clue you in on how to "smother" it. Smothering is a term used quite often in south Louisiana and it really means to cook vegetables, meats or seafood in their own juices (with some other seasonings) until they have "cooked down." The best way to explain this cooking method may be to describe to you how it's done.

But, first, here's one of my smothered okra stories.

The day began with a perfect sunrise. I am usually not an early riser, but, as luck would have it, my eyes popped open at 5:30 a.m. on the second day of my vacation. I knew sleep would not come again.

By the time the coffee brewed, the sun was creeping up across the bayou and the first golden rays touched the silky corn plants in the fields and sparkled the dew on the front lawn. In the distance I heard the whirring sound of a lawn mower and caught a whiff of freshly cut grass.

From my perch on the patio, I observed the red birds, squirrels and egrets heralding a new day. My reverie was disturbed by the ringing of the telephone. It was Aunt Lois.

"You want some fresh okra from my garden? I have more than I need. You don't even have to pick it. If you come now I'll give you a bucket full."

After I returned home, I realized that I had bitten off more than I could chew, smother or pickle.

I enlisted Mama to help. She arrived with her largest roasting pan under her arm and her favorite okra-cutting knife, and in no time we had the okra cooking.

Once the okra is cooked it can be packed in containers to store in the freezer. It's ideal to serve as a side dish or to use in gumbos. Oh, I must warn you: Don't cook okra in a cast iron pot – the okra will turn black.

Smothered Okra

Makes about 10 servings

4 quarts of fresh, sliced okra
3 large yellow onions, chopped
2 large green bell peppers, seeded and chopped
2 cans (16 ounces each) of whole tomatoes, crushed, with their liquid
1½ cups of vegetable oil
Salt and cayenne, to taste
¾ cup of water or chicken broth

Preheat the oven to 425 degrees.

In a large roasting pot, alternately layer the okra, onions, bell peppers, crushed tomatoes and juice, oil, salt and cayenne, and water or broth until all of the ingredients are used.

Cover the pot and place it in the preheated oven. Cook for 30 minutes, stir, and reduce the oven temperature to 350 degrees. Cover the pot and continue to cook for 2 to 2½ hours, stirring every 30 minutes. When the okra is no longer stringy, you'll know it is cooked.

Remove the pot from the oven and cool. Chill the okra well before you package it for the freezer.

Those darn hurricanes

Probably the only unfortunate aspect of living along the coastline of the Gulf of Mexico is the threat of hurricanes, most of which occur during the summer and early fall.

In 1992, Hurricane Andrew plowed through south Louisiana. For several days following the storm, Rock and I did little other than clear the yard of debris amid the relentless sounds of electric generators and chain saws.

Across the bayou from our house the willow trees that once swayed in the early morning breeze were reduced to nothing more than a clump of smashed and broken branches. The back yard, once cool and shady, was treeless.

For the most part, we survived with only some roof damage on the main house, but my small office, located in the back yard, was demolished. I was thanking my lucky stars and massaging my sore, aching muscles a week later when my friend Caroline arrived. She walked up the driveway carrying a basket of fresh herbs that made it through the storm. She pulled out a handful of basil, a bunch of thyme, a few sprigs of oregano, and a branch of rosemary.

"No matter what," she smiled, "we have to eat."

I gave her a big hug. A quick trip to the store got me the ingredients for a super supper.

Marinated Vegetables with Basil

Makes 6 servings

1 small head of broccoli
1 small head of cauliflower
3 medium carrots
1 small red onion
¾ cup of olive oil
1 tablespoon of Dijon mustard
½ teaspoon of fresh lemon juice
1 teaspoon of sugar
3 tablespoons of chopped fresh basil leaves
Salt and freshly ground black pepper, to taste

Blanch the broccoli and cauliflower for two to three minutes in boiling water. Drain and rinse with cold water. Break the broccoli into small florets and dry thoroughly.

Cut the carrots into thick slices, slice the onion and separate into rings, and place in a large bowl.

Whisk the oil, mustard, lemon juice, sugar and basil in a small bowl. Season with salt and pepper and pour over the vegetables.

Cover and refrigerate; stir occasionally.

Tomato, Corn & Bean Salad with Tarragon

Makes 4 servings

1 cup of whole-kernel corn, cooked and cooled
½ pound of green beans, cooked and cooled
3 medium-size tomatoes, chopped
2 tablespoons of finely chopped green onions (green part only)
1 teaspoon of chopped fresh tarragon leaves
Salt and freshly ground black pepper, to taste
1 tablespoon of chopped fresh parsley leaves

Toss all ingredients in a bowl and chill for at least an hour before serving.

My grandfather, Popete Broussard, gives my brother, Henri Clay, a ride on his shoulders in 1942.

Marinated Chicken with Thyme

Makes 4 servings

4 chicken breasts (6 ounces each), skinned and boned
Salt and freshly ground black pepper, to taste
¼ cup of soy sauce
4 tablespoons of honey
2 tablespoons of chicken broth
1 garlic clove, minced
2 teaspoons of chopped fresh thyme leaves
½ teaspoon of ground ginger
Pineapple chunks
Fresh thyme sprigs

Preheat the oven to 350 degrees.

Put the chicken breasts, sides tucked under and rolled slightly into a neat shape, in a glass dish. Season with salt and pepper.

Combine the soy sauce, honey, broth, garlic, thyme and ginger in a small bowl and whisk to blend. Cover the chicken with the mixture. Cover and refrigerate for at least an hour.

Remove from the refrigerator and bake for about 45 minutes or until the juices run clear. Garnish with pineapple chunks and fresh thyme leaves.

There's no substitute for a sandy beach

Louisiana is sometimes called the Bayou State because of the web of waterways crisscrossing the land. It also has its share of lakes and streams and, of course, it's bounded on the south by the Gulf of Mexico. Despite all this water, the state has little in the way of beaches. Instead of white sand, we have mud and marsh.

When I just have to dig my toes in the sand, I head east, to the sandy beaches along the Mississippi Gulf Coast and, perhaps, beyond to Florida. When time is short, I make a quick getaway to Mobile, well, really to Point Clear, Alabama, on the shores of Mobile Bay.

During a three-day respite one summer at The Grand Hotel at Point Clear, I did not do much other than lounge on the small beach overlooking the gray-green water. It was mind-clearing time and I just wanted to be lazy.

One afternoon, a groundskeeper who was tending the already manicured lawn near my spot asked me if I knew about "Jubilee."

I asked if it had anything to do with the highway span that crosses Mobile Bay being called Jubilee something or other.

"Yes, it sure does!" he replied. And he told me this story.

A phenomenon occurs, mostly during the summer, when a combination of thousands of crabs, fish and shrimp come right up on shore.

People who quickly gather after the first cry of "Jubilee" have no trouble at all filling buckets, baskets and sacks with the delicacies of the deep.

Despite the inconvenient hour (Jubilees happen at night, often between midnight and dawn.) it takes no time at all for a crowd to gather.

Sometimes it's primarily flounders that congregate; other times it's shrimp or crabs. But, generally, all three species are involved.

Jubilees have not been positively explained by science, but two theories exist based upon the changing bay water. Some believe that the fish and shellfish may be dazed by a sudden merging of fresh and salt water. Others believe it's caused by changing temperatures of the water following heavy rains.

Finishing his story and his work, the groundskeeper went on his way.

What a tale! I thought about it on my drive home and resolved to fix a "jubilee" dinner in honor of this event.

Childhood friend Jack Nugier plays on the beach at Grand Isle around 1950, right after a storm came through. Note the storm damage in the background.

Family and friends enjoy the surf at Grand Isle around 1950. That's Henri Clay at left, and to his right is Mama holding me. The others in the picture are our friends.

Stuffed Crab Jubilee

Makes 6 servings

2 slices of bacon
½ cup of chopped yellow onions
½ cup of chopped celery
¼ cup of chopped green bell peppers
1 pound of lump crabmeat, picked over for
    shells and cartilage
1 clove of garlic, minced
1 large egg, beaten
¼ cup of milk
1 stick (8 tablespoons) of butter or
    margarine, melted
2 tablespoons of chopped fresh parsley
    leaves
1 teaspoon of dry mustard
½ teaspoon of salt
¼ teaspoon of cayenne
1 teaspoon of Worcestershire sauce
½ cup of Italian-style bread crumbs

Preheat oven to 350 degrees.
Fry the bacon, drain on paper towels, and crumble. Set aside.

Reserve the drippings in the skillet. Add the onions, celery and bell peppers and cook, stirring, until they are wilted, about three minutes. Remove from the heat.

In a mixing bowl, combine the bacon and cooked vegetables with the rest of the ingredients and toss to mix well.

Stuff the mixture into clean crab shells or put it into a casserole dish. Bake uncovered for 15 minutes.

Skewered Shrimp with Zucchini

Makes 4 to 6 servings

2 pounds of medium-size shrimp, peeled and deveined
2 medium-size zucchini, thinly sliced into rounds
3 tablespoons of soy sauce
2 cloves of garlic, mashed
1/2 teaspoon of ground ginger
1/8 teaspoon of Tabasco
2 tablespoons of olive oil
Pinch of sugar

Mix the shrimp and zucchini with the rest of the ingredients and marinate in the refrigerator for one hour.

Alternately skewer the shrimp and zucchini slices and cook on a hot grill; baste with the marinade frequently. Cook three to five minutes per side or until cooked through.

Fourth of July fare

The Fourth of July is probably the quintessential American holiday and the only big holiday of the summer season. It's always a grand excuse to have a party with friends and relatives.

At picnics in the back yard, by the pool, at the camp, or on the patio, the Fourth can be as simple or as fancy as you want it to be. All-American food like hot dogs, hamburgers, fried chicken, cole slaw, potato salad and lots of ice cold watermelon are hard to beat.

Papa's birthday was July 6 and a niece, Suzanne, was born on July 7, so the holiday is indeed a celebration for us. With our family still growing (We're now into great grandchildren.), the party is a *mélange* of people and of food. We still gather at the camp on Catahoula Lake, but now each family is responsible for their own food. You wouldn't believe the assortment of dishes that sometimes appear on the large picnic tables! What follows is merely a sampling of the incredible array.

Cobb salad was made famous at Hollywood's Brown Derby, but one of the grandsons came up with the idea of making a Cobb club sandwich. This is his take on it:

Cobb Club Sandwich

Makes 4 servings

4 large pita breads
2 tablespoons of Creole mustard or any whole-grain mustard
2 tablespoons of mayonnaise
½ head of green leaf lettuce, cleaned and finely chopped
1 bunch of watercress, cleaned and stemmed
2 tablespoons of minced green onions or chives
2 medium tomatoes, chopped
2 cooked chicken breasts, diced
6 slices of bacon, crisply cooked and crumbled
1 medium avocado, peeled, chopped and sprinkled with a teaspoon of fresh lemon juice
2 hard-boiled eggs, finely chopped
½ cup of crumbled Roquefort cheese

Spread the inside of the pita pockets with the mustard and mayonnaise. Divide the lettuce into four equal portions and make a layer on one side of each pocket. Continue to layer the watercress, green onions, tomatoes, chicken, bacon, avocado, eggs and cheese.

This bread and the following corn bread recipes were contributed by another grandchild, our free spirit!

Zucchini Spice Bread

Makes 2 loaves

3 cups of grated zucchini
¾ cup of vegetable oil
1 cup of honey
4 large eggs, beaten
2 teaspoons of vanilla extract
3 cups of whole-wheat flour
1 teaspoon of baking soda
1 teaspoon of baking powder
1 teaspoon of salt
1 teaspoon of nutmeg
1 tablespoon of cinnamon
1 cup of raisins or chopped nuts

Preheat the oven to 350 degrees.

Mix the ingredients in the order listed. Pour the batter into two greased 9x5-inch loaf pans and bake for 45 minutes or until they spring back when touched.

Remove the loaves from the oven and set on wire racks to cool. Cover with a clean cloth. When completely cool, remove the loaves from the pan.

If you wish to freeze the loaves, put them in freezer bags. When ready to use, defrost and warm in the oven.

Red Pepper Corn Bread

Makes 6 servings

2 tablespoons of bacon fat or vegetable oil
1 cup of yellow cornmeal
1 cup of all-purpose flour
2½ teaspoons of baking powder
1 teaspoon of salt
½ teaspoon of baking soda
½ cup of chopped red bell peppers
½ cup of chopped green onions (green part only)
1 tablespoon of chopped pickled jalapeño peppers
½ cup of plain yogurt
½ cup of milk
1 large egg
½ stick (4 tablespoons) of butter, melted
¼ cup of grated Monterey Jack cheese

Preheat the oven to 400 degrees.

Oil a 10-inch cast-iron skillet or a 9-inch square baking pan with the bacon fat or vegetable oil. Mix together the cornmeal, flour, baking powder, salt and baking soda in a mixing bowl. Add the bell peppers, green onions and jalapeños, and mix.

In a small bowl, whisk together the yogurt, milk and egg. Add this mixture and the butter to the dry ingredients and stir to mix.

Pour the mixture into the skillet or pan, sprinkle with cheese, and bake uncovered for about 30 minutes or until golden brown. Serve immediately.

My nieces and nephews play in the baby pool in 1978. Left to right are Becki, Andrea and Ben Landry; and Marti and Nicole Bienvenu.

Deep red ripe tomatoes brighten up any table and are perfect for a Fourth of July spread.

Stuffed Tomatoes

Makes 8 servings

8 medium-size tomatoes
Salt and freshly ground black pepper, to taste
2 large eggs
2 tablespoons of all-purpose flour
2 tablespoons of sugar
½ teaspoon of baking powder
1 cup of half-and-half
1 cup of fresh corn kernels
2 tablespoons of butter, melted
Chopped fresh parsley leaves

Preheat the oven to 350 degrees.

Slice off and discard the tops of the tomatoes. Scoop out the pulp and seeds. Sprinkle the tomato shells with salt and pepper. Invert the tomatoes on paper towels and drain for about 10 minutes.

Beat the eggs in a mixing bowl. Add the flour, sugar, baking powder and half-and-half and stir-in the corn and the butter. Season with salt and black pepper.

Spoon the mixture into the tomatoes and put the tomatoes into the individual compartments of a lightly oiled muffin tin. Bake until the custard is puffed, lightly browned, and firm to the touch, about 45 minutes.

Sprinkle the tops of the tomatoes with parsley to serve.

Having fun at their Uncle Henri and Aunt Maria's house around 1982 are, left to right, my cousin's children, Jeremy and Jennifer LeBlanc, nephew Gerard Bienvenu and niece Suzanne Bienvenu (kneeling). Standing are nephew Ben Landry and niece Nicole Bienvenu.

My mother adores figs, which are at their peak right around the Fourth of July. This scrumptious ice cream is made every year in her honor.

Fig & Grand Marnier Ice Cream

Makes about 1½ quarts

1 quart of ripe figs, peeled and mashed
½ cup of Grand Marnier
6 large eggs, lightly beaten
4 cups of milk
1 cup of sugar
1 tablespoon of pure vanilla extract

Combine the figs and Grand Marnier in a bowl and set aside.

In a large, heavy, nonreactive saucepan, combine the eggs, milk, sugar and vanilla over medium heat and whisk to dissolve sugar. Bring to a gentle boil, stirring constantly, then reduce heat to medium-low. Continue stirring until the mixture thickens enough to coat a wooden spoon.

Remove from heat and let cool for about 10 minutes. Cover and refrigerate until well chilled.

Add the fig mixture and stir to mix. Pour the mixture into an ice cream freezer and freeze according to the manufacturer's directions.

Local blackberries that grow wild along fences have long been used in desserts around here, but in recent years several blueberry farms have sprung up in the area, and we've been experimenting with these plump berries. This recipe is a new one in our dessert repertoire for summer celebrations.

Lemon Curd with Blueberries

Makes 6 to 8 servings

1 1/3 cups of sugar
1 3/4 sticks of butter
2/3 cup of fresh lemon juice
4 large eggs
4 egg yolks
1 tablespoon of grated lemon peel
4 cups of fresh blueberries, rinsed and
   picked over

Whisk the sugar, butter, lemon juice, eggs, egg yolks and lemon peel in the top of a non-reactive double boiler set over boiling water until the mixture thickens enough to coat the back of a spoon. Do not let the mixture boil.

Transfer the mixture to a glass container and cool to room temperature. Cover and refrigerate for at least four hours before using.

Fill parfait glasses with alternate layers of the lemon curd and berries. Chill for 30 minutes before serving.

Living on the bayou

Living on a bayou, especially a charming one like Bayou Teche, certainly has its perks. Rock and I take full advantage of it during the summer months when the days are long and lazy.

One evening when I arrived home from work, Rock's van was in the driveway, lights were on in the house, and I could hear Harry Connick Jr. crooning from the tape deck on the patio.

"Honey, I'm home," I called out.

No answer. I made a quick tour of the cottage and found notes tacked here and there.

One read, "I've gone for a ride in the boat." Another simply said, "Bullets for supper. Ground meat in the refrigerator is seasoned."

Lined up on the kitchen counter was a jar of olives, a basket of small fresh mushrooms, several pods of peeled garlic in a saucer, and several potatoes, peeled and floating in a bowl of cool water. A can of peas and a small loaf of French bread rounded out the tableau.

I laughed. It appeared that Rock had his mouth set for good old meatballs, called *boulettes* around here, or as Rock dubs them, "bullets."

From the kitchen window I could see Rock zipping up and down in his boat having a grand time. I set about my task hoping that I would be rewarded with a moonlight ride down the bayou.

Boulettes

Makes 10 to 12 meatballs

1 pound of lean ground beef
1 pound of lean ground pork
½ teaspoon of cayenne
1½ teaspoons of salt
1 tablespoon of Worcestershire sauce
¼ teaspoon of garlic powder
12 small white button mushrooms,
    or 12 pitted olives *or* 12 garlic pods
1 tablespoon of olive oil
1 cup of beef broth

Season the ground beef and pork with the cayenne, salt, Worcestershire sauce and garlic powder. Form the meat into large meatballs. In the center of each meatball, poke either a pod of garlic, an olive or a mushroom.

In a deep iron skillet, heat the olive oil and brown the meatballs; add the beef broth, cover, and reduce heat to medium-low. Cook for 20 to 25 minutes, or until the juices run clear.

Creamy Creamed Potatoes

Makes 4 servings

4 medium red potatoes, peeled
4 tablespoons of melted butter or margarine
1/2 cup of grated American or
    cheddar cheese
1 large egg, beaten
1/3 cup of warm evaporated milk
Salt and white pepper, to taste

Boil the potatoes in water until fork-tender. Drain and return to the pot and mash with a fork.

Combine the mashed potatoes with the rest of the ingredients, adding warm milk until the mixture is smooth. Season to taste and serve immediately.

All was ready when Rock opened the screen door to the kitchen. He suggested we take our supper outside on trays and picnic in the boat on the bayou by the light of the silvery moon. What an evening!

Another boat excursion we took together was not so lovely.

One year we made arrangements with another couple to rent a houseboat for a long weekend at Pass Christian, Mississippi. The four of us made our lists. Since we were told that the boat was air-conditioned, had a microwave, and had a real shower, we felt we would be in the lap of luxury.

We packed a linen tablecloth and napkins, votive candles, good plastic ware, and wine glasses in a fine picnic basket. Three bottles of Pinot Noir and two of Muscadet were thrown in for good measure. Our evening meals would be enjoyed while we anchored in safe waters.

The men packed folding chairs for the sundeck and a small barbecue grill. Rock had his fishing gear and his favorite Hawaiian shirt. Pat had his sailing cap and a couple of starched white shirts. Cute group!

At dawn on the day of departure, thunderstorms rolled through as we packed the Jeep. We assured one another that the weather would blow over by the time we hit the Mississippi Gulf Coast.

It was raining when we arrived at the marina. It was raining as we motored down the Jordan River. It was storming when we passed under the bridge at The Pass and headed out to the channel, but we were doing fine until we were about 50 yards from the Pass Christian Yacht Club. The engine went dead.

We threw out the anchor, hunkered

down and notified the marina and the Coast Guard. Since we were not in danger, we were told to just sit tight.

The storm finally ended and we were able to grill our steaks, make a big salad, and sip our wine. During the night, another storm came up, and it was the first time I wished there were seat belts on a bed!

When we were rescued and towed in the next morning, it was still raining. But our spirits were not dampened. We moved to another boat and, during the reloading, my friend Jeri and I bought a few pounds of shrimp off a shrimp boat docked near us. We had a feast that evening.

Marinated Grilled Shrimp

Makes 4 servings

4 pounds of large shrimp, unpeeled
1 stick (8 tablespoons) of butter, melted
4 tablespoons of olive oil
1 medium yellow onion, thinly sliced
1 small green bell pepper, seeded and thinly sliced
4 cloves of garlic, minced
3 tablespoons of fresh lemon juice
1 teaspoon of dried rosemary leaves
1 tablespoon of minced fresh parsley leaves
1 tablespoon of sweet paprika
2 tablespoons of Worcestershire sauce
Salt, cayenne, and freshly ground black pepper, to taste (don't be stingy)
¼ cup of dry white wine

Place the shrimp in a large glass dish.

Combine all of the other ingredients and pour over the shrimp. Marinate in the refrigerator for two to four hours.

When you are ready to grill, remove the shrimp from the marinade and place in a grilling basket. Grill over a medium-hot fire for 10 minutes, turning the grill basket two or three times to cook evenly.

Shrimp Casserole

Makes 6 servings

2 pounds of medium-size shrimp, peeled and deveined, heads and shells reserved
4 tablespoons of butter or margarine
2 tablespoons of all-purpose flour
½ cup of milk
½ cup of shrimp stock (made from shrimp shells)
½ cup of chopped green onion (green part only)
1 cup of sliced fresh white mushrooms
8 ounces of Monterey Jack cheese, cubed
2 tablespoons of dry vermouth
Salt and cayenne, to taste
1 pound of capellini pasta, cooked and drained
1 cup of grated cheddar cheese

Preheat the oven to 350 degrees.

Put the shrimp heads and shells into a stockpot, cover with water, and boil for 30 minutes. Cool, strain, and reserve the stock.

Melt the butter in a saucepan over low heat. Add the flour, stirring until blended and smooth, but not brown. Add the milk and shrimp stock slowly, stirring constantly. Cook until smooth and thick.

Add the green onions, mushrooms, and shrimp and cook until the shrimp turn pink. Add the Monterey Jack and vermouth and continue stirring until the cheese melts and the sauce is smooth. Season with salt and pepper.

Place the cooked pasta in a casserole dish and cover the pasta with the shrimp sauce. Top with the cheddar cheese and bake uncovered for 15 minutes or until the sauce bubbles. Serve immediately.

Displaying our catch of the day at Grand Isle in 2006 are Rock and me on the left and our friends, Pat and Margaret Caffery.

Vacationing on the Gulf Coast

When Rock and I go on summer vacations to Florida, he shakes his head when I pack everything but the kitchen sink. He explains to me that we're not going to a foreign country, that there are supermarkets everywhere, and that it would be simpler to do our grocery shopping once we're there. Do I listen? No way.

In the ice chest, a very large one, go a couple of packs of frozen shrimp that have been stashed in the freezer, a bag of home-grown tomatoes, and maybe some sausage and an assortment of jams and jellies. You just never know!

Poor Rock, by the time we leave our vehicle is packed to the roof, not only with the makings for several meals, but with beach chairs and umbrellas, floaties, beach towels, clothes, magazines and books, a

jam box (large portable radio) and a collection of tapes.

One particular summer, arrangements were made to join several other couples in Orange Beach, Alabama. After unloading our "stuff" into the respective condominiums, we gathered to make plans. Someone was to get the sailboat readied, another was appointed to blow up all the floaties, and meal assignments were made. One rule was agreed upon: There were no rules. "Eat, drink and be merry" was our war cry.

One night we dined on perfectly baked ham, roasted chicken, pasta and shrimp, and giant wedges of peach pie. Another evening we gorged on baked brisket and baked potatoes. Another feast included grilled grouper and rib eye steaks. One must keep up one's strength to play in the surf, lounge on the beach, and ply the waters in a sailboat!

On the day before departure, we took it a little easier and voted for a late brunch. Whoever gave birth to the idea of brunch had the right idea. It can be served anywhere from 10 a.m. to 2 p.m. It can begin with Bloody Marys or Mimosas, mint juleps, or cups of *cafe au lait*, or tall glasses of ice tea garnished with fresh mint sprigs.

This was our menu:

Griddle Cakes

Makes about 12 cakes

3/4 cup of all-purpose flour
3/4 cup of yellow cornmeal
1 tablespoon of sugar
1 1/2 teaspoons of baking powder
1/2 teaspoon of salt
2 large egg yolks
1 1/3 cups of milk
2 tablespoons of melted butter
2 egg whites, beaten into stiff peaks
Vegetable oil

Sift together in a bowl the flour, cornmeal, sugar, baking powder and salt. Make a well in the center of the dry ingredients.

In a separate bowl, beat together the egg yolks and milk. Add to the dry ingredients and beat until well blended and smooth. Stir in the melted butter. Gently fold in the beaten egg whites.

Brush a hot griddle or skillet with the oil.

Pour the batter onto the hot griddle or skillet in small pools about four inches in diameter. Turn the griddle cakes as they become fluffy and full of bubbles. Turn only once.

Serve with butter and warm syrup.

Sausage Corn Bread Pie

Makes 6 servings

1 pound of fresh pork sausage, removed from the casing and crumbled
1 cup of yellow cornmeal
1 cup of all-purpose flour
¼ cup of sugar
4 teaspoons of baking soda
1 large egg
1 cup of milk

Preheat the oven to 425 degrees.

Cook the sausage in a large skillet until all pink in the meat disappears. Pour off the drippings, reserving about three tablespoons.

Sift together the cornmeal, flour, sugar and baking powder. Add the egg, milk and pan drippings. Mix together and fold in the sausage.

Turn the batter into a greased 9-inch pie pan. Bake for about 25 minutes or until set.

Cool for about three minutes before slicing to serve.

Ju-Ju's Buttermilk Biscuits

Makes 8 servings

3 cups of all-purpose flour
3 tablespoons of baking powder
1 teaspoon of salt
1 stick (8 tablespoons) of cold unsalted butter
1½ cups of buttermilk

Preheat the oven to 400 degrees.

Combine all the dry ingredients in a mixing bowl; use your fingers to cut in the butter until you have a coarse meal. Add the buttermilk and stir with a fork to produce a dough.

Knead the dough lightly on a floured

That's me in the summer of 2005, having a good laugh during the cocktail hour at Grand Isle.

board. Roll it out to approximately 1/2 inch thick and cut into rounds with a biscuit cutter.

Place the biscuits on a cookie sheet and bake for 8 to 10 minutes, until golden brown.

In Kentucky, on what is known as Derby Day, mint juleps are the order of the day. But here in the South, juleps are enjoyed throughout the hot months when fresh mint just about takes over the garden. There's nothing quite like a tall, cold julep to soothe a parched mouth.

For centuries the julep has been de-scribed as "something to cool or assuage the heat of passion" or "a sweet drink prepared in different ways." The earli-est form of the word was *iulep*. Arabs called it *julab*, the Portuguese *julepe*, the Italians *giulebbe*. The Latins named it *julapium* and the Persians *gul-ab*, mean-ing "rose water." "Julep" is the way we spell it is French.

According to the experts, it's best not to use rye whiskey in making a julep. If you do use whiskey, use bourbon. There are many kinds of mint juleps, with each Southern state claiming a different variety. Although Georgia may be able to make good the boast that the mint ju-lep originated within her borders, there appear to be no successful refutations of Kentucky's claim that the Blue Grass State popularized the famous drink.

Whatever. It doesn't matter to me from whence it came; I only know that I do enjoy them on a scorching afternoon. Although there are many recipes and methods, this is one that I prefer.

My Mint Julep

Makes 1 drink

1 dozen fresh mint leaves plus
   2 sprigs of fresh mint
1 teaspoon of sugar
2 ounces of bourbon
1 ounce of dark rum
Finely crushed ice

Put the mint leaves in a tall glass. Add the sugar and, with a spoon, crush the leaves and stir. Pour in the bourbon and the rum.

Fill the glass with the ice, then juggle (don't stir) until the outside of the glass is heavily frosted. Garnish with the mint sprigs.

'The Grill Master'

My husband Rock likes to grill and barbecue. It's important to know that there is a difference between the two, although sometimes the terms are used interchangeably. To grill is to prepare food on a grill over hot coals or another heat source, and the product to be cooked is close to the fire, as in grilling hamburgers, hot dogs, steaks and fish. This procedure is usually a fairly quick one, while to barbecue is to prepare food that uses lower temperatures and no direct flames. Hot smoke does the cooking, gradually adding its own flavor to the meat, which remains naturally moist. (There is also a smoking process by which a product is slow-cooked, with the fire being away from the product, but we need not go into that here.)

Think of it this way: Grilling is "fast" food; barbecue is "slow" food.

But back to my story. Rock likes to do both, more often in the summer, but the season really doesn't matter to him. I've watched him barbecue chicken and pork ribs in the dead of winter bundled up in a wool coat with a fur-lined hunting cap scrunched down over his ears.

But more often than not, we grill all year-round. For about eight years, Rock grilled on a very small pit, which could accommodate at one time little more than two steaks or four fish fillets, or six hamburgers. I offered many times to get him a more substantial one – a pit with which he could grill, barbecue and smoke. But he adamantly refused, explaining that "Little Red" does quite nicely, thank you.

His knack for grilling and barbecue earned him the name of "Grill Master" by our friends, neighbors and relatives. He says he learned all that he knows from his father, Papa Rock, who had his very own outdoor kitchen where he

My husband, Rock Lasserre, at the helm of his boat in the summer of 2000.

fixed meals not only for his family but for a great wealth of friends.

Rock has become renowned for his steaks, pork tenders, hamburgers, chicken breasts, kabobs of all kinds, grilled seafood, and assorted vegetables. His marinades and basting sauces are legendary. Why, even the neighborhood children hold him in high regard and won't let anyone else roast their wieners.

But finally "Little Red" met its demise. One evening I came home to find that Rock, who arrived earlier than I, had cleaned the patio, raked down by the bayou where silt had accumulated during a downpour, and fluffed up the canvas chairs in the yard.

The weather was nearly perfect, warm, but with a cool breeze stirring the branches of the trees. He went to retrieve his little red pit from the garage. I was foraging around for the makings for a Salty Dog (vodka and grapefruit juice) when I heard a loud groan.

I went to the screen door that led to the garage and found Rock on the steps cradling the little pit. At first I was a bit concerned. I thought perhaps he had dropped the darn thing on his foot. Then I realized that the bottom had rusted out and the grill was in pieces.

He looked up at me teary-eyed.

"Miss B., do you know how many evenings we've spent with this thing and how much good food it has cooked for us? And now it's gone!"

I gently took it from his arms and buried it near the wood pile. I gave Rock some money from the pizza jar and suggested he go out and find a new one. Within an hour he was home again with another pit, a bit larger than "Little Red," and he was ready to go.

Here are a few recipes from his repertoire.

Grilled Redfish

Makes 2 servings

2 redfish (or any firm white fish such as grouper, trout, or redfish) each about 8 ounces (leave scales on)
2 tablespoons of vegetable oil
Salt and cayenne, to taste
4 tablespoons of margarine, melted
2 tablespoons of fresh lime juice
1 tablespoon of Lea & Perrins Marinade for Chicken
1 teaspoon of paprika

Prepare the grill.

Rub the fillets with the vegetable oil and season with salt and cayenne.

In a small saucepan, combine the margarine, lime juice, marinade and paprika.

Put the fillets on the grill, scale side down, over a medium fire. Dab them with some of the basting sauce and close the lid. Cook for two to three minutes.

Dab again with the basting sauce, close the lid and cook for three to five minutes, or until the fish flakes easily with a fork.

When serving, drizzle the fish with the remaining basting sauce.

Grilled Marinated Flank Steaks

Makes 4 servings

¼ cup of apple cider vinegar
¼ cup of Worcestershire sauce
3 tablespoons of Tabasco
2 tablespoons of margarine
2 tablespoons of olive oil
1 teaspoon of brown sugar
2 pounds of flank steak
1 teaspoon of fresh rosemary leaves, with woody stems reserved

Combine the first six ingredients in a saucepan and bring to a boil, stirring until the sugar dissolves; cool.

Place the steak in a shallow glass or ceramic dish. Pour the marinade over the meat, cover, and refrigerate for three hours, turning occasionally.

Make a hot fire in the grill. (When Rock has rosemary stems, he throws these on the fire.)

Drain the steaks, reserving the marinade. Grill the steaks four to five minutes on each side for medium-rare and baste with marinade.

Slice the steak thinly across the grain. Garnish with rosemary leaves.

Grilled Shrimp with Smoked Sausage & Basil

Makes 4 appetizer servings

24 large shrimp, peeled and deveined
   (leave tails on)
½ pound of smoked sausage,
   cut crosswise into 1/4-inch slices
3 tablespoons of olive oil
1 tablespoon of balsamic vinegar
½ teaspoon of salt
¼ teaspoon of cayenne
2 tablespoons of finely chopped fresh
   basil leaves

Thread the shrimp and sausage alternately on skewers. Brush the shrimp and sausage with the olive oil and vinegar. Season with salt and cayenne.

Grill over a medium-hot fire for about five minutes, or until the shrimp turn pink and firm.

Remove and sprinkle with the basil.

Rock likes nothing better than "surf and turf," and most of the time he indulges and serves his turf with steamed lobsters from the supermarket. But sometimes he will use shrimp for his "surf."

Rock's Surf & Turf

Makes 2 servings

SURF

 6 large shrimp, deheaded, peeled, deveined,
   and butterflied
1 cup of lump crabmeat, picked over for
   shells and cartilage
6 tablespoons of clarified butter
1 tablespoon of finely chopped green onions
   (green part only)
1 tablespoon of crushed almonds
1/8 teaspoon of Lea & Perrins
   Marinade for Chicken
1 teaspoon of capers, drained
Salt and white pepper, to taste

In a small skillet, toss the shrimp and crabmeat in the butter over low heat until the shrimp turn pink.

Add the green onions, almonds, marinade, capers, salt and pepper. Toss gently for two to three minutes.

Serve on toast points.

TURF

2 beef tenderloin filets (6 ounces each)
2 tablespoons of olive oil
¼ teaspoon of ground oregano
¼ teaspoon of garlic powder
Salt and freshly ground black pepper,
   to taste
2 tablespoons of dry red wine

Rub the steaks with the oil and dry seasonings. Heat a large skillet over medium heat, add the steaks and cook for three minutes on each side for medium-rare, or four to five minutes for medium. Remove the steaks to a warm platter. Add the wine to the skillet and stir to loosen any browned bits. Cook for one minute.

Pour the pan drippings over the steaks to serve.

My husband is full of surprises. I never know what he's going to do – which makes for some frustrating times, but then there is never a dull moment.

For instance, read this story about the barbecued chicken.

One Wednesday evening while driving down the lane to our house, I noticed a cloud of smoke hovering over the neighborhood. My first thought was that someone was burning leaves, but I took a deep whiff and realized that it was the scent of barbecue tingling my nose. I pulled in to our driveway, and through the haze of smoke I saw Rock standing before a large pit with a happy grin on his face.

"What's up, Rocky Docky? Is tonight your annual office party? Did I miss something?

"Calm yourself, Miss B. I just had a hankering to barbecue so I borrowed the neighbor's pit and I'm having a blast!" he retorted.

With great aplomb he threw open the cover of the pit. There on the grill were six halves of chicken, several pounds of thick pork chops, and a few links of fresh pork sausage, more than enough to feed a hungry baseball team.

"Why so much?" I calmly asked.

"Well, look at it this way. You won't have to cook for the next several days," said the king of leftovers.

Since he appeared to have everything under control, I didn't bother to ask if he needed any help. Plus, he was having so much fun I didn't want to interrupt his project. I went about my business. I worked in the flower beds, washed a couple of loads of laundry, and went through a stack of newspapers that had piled up on my desk.

All the while he gave me his philosophy on barbecuing.

First of all, one shouldn't quarter the chickens. They should only be cut in half. Otherwise they tend to get dry. An electric or gas grill simply will not do. It must be a charcoal fire. The fire must be about 15 to 18 inches from the grill. Cook the chicken low and slow. The sausage and pork chops should be put along the outer edges of the grill as they will cook too quickly over direct heat. The basting sauce is his father's recipe.

Rock's Barbecued Chicken

Makes 6 servings

3 plump fryers, cut in half
2 tablespoons of Creole or Cajun seasoning
1 stick (8 tablespoons) of margarine
1 bottle (6 ounces) of Tabasco

Rub the chickens well with the seasoning. Melt the margarine in a small saucepan and add the Tabasco.

Put the chickens on the grill and baste frequently with the sauce. Be sure to turn the chickens every 20 minutes. Keep the cover of the barbecue pit closed when not turning or basting the chickens. The chickens will take about 2½ hours to cook.

Rock is not limited to grilling and barbecuing. He does a darn good job with other things, like these two red snapper recipes.

If you don't have Creole tomatoes, use whatever tomatoes you have. Just be sure they are good and ripe.

Redfish & Creole Tomatoes

Makes 6 servings

2 tablespoons of olive oil
6 redfish or trout fillets (6 to 8 ounces each)
2 tablespoons of soy sauce
¼ teaspoon of cayenne
2 tablespoons of chopped green onions
   (green part only)
2 tablespoons of chopped fresh
   parsley leaves
2 tablespoons of fresh lemon juice
3 tablespoons of butter or margarine, melted
Onion-Tomato Sauce (Recipe follows)

Preheat the broiler.

Line a shallow pan with aluminum foil. Spread the olive oil evenly in the pan and add the fillets, turning them to evenly coat with the oil.

Season both sides of the fillets with the soy sauce and cayenne. Sprinkle the fillets with the green onions, parsley, lemon juice and butter.

Broil for four to six minutes or until the fish flakes easily with a fork.

Top with the Onion-Tomato Sauce and serve immediately.

ONION-TOMATO SAUCE

3 tablespoons of olive oil
1½ cups of thinly sliced Vidalia or other
   sweet onions
1 cup of thinly sliced green or red
   bell peppers
1 cup of chopped tomatoes, preferably
   Creole tomatoes
½ teaspoon of salt
¼ teaspoon of cayenne
Pinch of sugar
2 teaspoons of apple cider vinegar

Heat the olive oil in a large skillet over medium heat. Add the onions and bell peppers and cook, stirring, for about two minutes, or until slightly limp.

Add the tomatoes and cook, stirring, for one minute. Add the salt, cayenne, sugar and vinegar and cook, stirring occasionally, for two minutes.

This next recipe has, naturally, a story behind it.

One of Rock's fishing buddies brought us a beautiful 8-pound red snapper one Friday evening. It was gutted, cleaned, with its head on, and ready to cook. Since we already had supper going, we packed the beauty on a bed of crushed ice in our large ice chest.

On Saturday, Rock informed me that the snapper was *his* fish and he was going to be in charge of cooking it. Hey, that was fine with me; have at it, buddy! I had plenty to keep me busy throughout the day. I gave him permission to use *my* library of seafood cookbooks to find the perfect recipe for *his* fish. All day long, I noticed him draining the ice chest and refilling it with fresh ice to keep *his* fish cool and happy. He even talked to *his* fish.

"Baby, you are going to be so delicious! I'm going to stuff you with fresh crabmeat and shrimp, rub you with herbs and spices and then bake you. How would you like that?"

For a minute, I wondered if Rock thought *his* fish would answer him.

By late afternoon, Rock had completed most of his preparations. When friends joined us for dinner, Rock was ready. He had borrowed a large pan from Mama, the table was set, a couple of bottles of white wine were chilling, and Jimmy Buffet crooned in the background.

Rock, swathed in a starched white apron with a chef's toque atop his head, rubbed his hands. We watched him gently remove *his* fish from the bed of ice and set it on a nest of clean towels on the countertop. He then proceeded to prepare *his* fish.

Rock's Red Snapper

Makes about 8 servings

One 8-pound red snapper, dressed
Salt and cayenne, to taste
1½ sticks of butter or margarine
1 cup of finely chopped yellow onions
½ cup of finely chopped celery
½ cup of finely chopped green bell peppers
2 garlic cloves, minced
1 pound of small shrimp, peeled
  and deveined
1 pound of lump or claw crabmeat, picked
  over for shells and cartilage
Pinch of dried oregano leaves
Pinch of dried thyme leaves
1 large egg
1½ cups of Italian bread crumbs
3 tablespoons of olive oil
4 tablespoons of fresh lemon juice
Lemon slices for garnish
Olives to put in the eyes of the snapper

Preheat the oven to 400 degrees.

Rub the fish well both inside and out with salt and cayenne. Set aside.

In a large skillet, melt one stick of the butter and add the onions, celery, bell peppers and garlic and sauté until transparent, about four minutes.

Add the shrimp and cook until they turn pink. Add the crabmeat and toss gently. Season with salt, cayenne, oregano and thyme. Add the egg and stir. Add the bread crumbs a little at a time until the stuffing becomes thick. Cool to room temperature.

Fill the cavity of the fish with the stuffing and secure with toothpicks. Combine the remaining four tablespoons of butter (melted), olive oil and lemon juice, and bathe the fish with this mixture.

Bake for 15 minutes and then baste again with the lemon-butter mixture. Reduce the oven temperature to 350 degrees and cook for about 45 minutes more or until the fish flakes easily with a fork.

Garnish with lemon slices and put olives in the eye sockets. Remove the toothpicks.

Serve a heaping tablespoonful of stuffing with pieces of fish.

Some of the men of our family gathered for a picture on Thanksgiving Day 1949.
Check out those styles! Left to right: my grandfather, Popete Broussard; my
father, Blackie Bienvenu; and my grandfather, Lazaire "Pop" Bienvenu.

FALL

It always makes me sad to bid *au revoir* to summer. I never seem to get enough of splashing in a swimming pool, playing in the sand at the beach, riding my bike in the neighborhood until dusk, or catching crabs from the wharf at Vermilion Bay. But, I must admit that when the first cool front blows in from the west, I feel a gush of energy.

The air is refreshed and it's a great time to ride around, with the car windows open, on the rural roads to check on the sugarcane crop before it's harvested. Tall and green, the heavy stalks of cane sway in the wind waiting to be harvested when cool weather moves in.

A flock of ducks flying in V-formation head south, quacking loudly, and I catch a whiff of burning leaves. The days are imperceptibly but relentlessly getting shorter, and the locals put up their summer whites and air out sweaters and jackets for the chill and change that is on the way.

The football season is in full swing and so is the hunting season. On weekends it's difficult to find a man on the streets: They're either at the stadium or at the hunting camp.

Cold weather sends everyone indoors, and there is no better time to make a big pot of gumbo or vegetable soup.

The spindly pecan trees shed their brown, crackly leaves, and the locals scramble to gather the nuts to use throughout the winter in pies, cakes and other Louisiana favorites.

When October rolls around, my nieces and nephews are quick to remind me of our annual Halloween party that is usually held at my home on the banks of

Bayou Teche. My witch costume is dragged out of storage and fluffed up. Invitations are sent out, and the menu is planned.

Before we know it, Thanksgiving is at hand and there will be many family gatherings for which to prepare.

Mais oui, mes amis, it's time to hunker down in front of a roaring fire and enjoy the season.

I love Halloween, and I've been known to dress up as a witch – but a friendly *witch! This picture was taken in 1995.*

My parents' 40th anniversary was in 1980. That's them seated. Standing (left to right): me; my brother Bruce and his wife Nancy; Maria and my brother Henri Clay; and my sister Edna and her husband Al Landry.

You can *go home again*

After living away from St. Martinville (my hometown) for some 25 years, I returned. It was good to be home again and after a few weeks I realized that not much had changed. Well, some things are still the same, but there are some that aren't.

My childhood playmate, Syl, now lives two houses down from me, so we can play together again just like we did when we were five years old. Mama still lives on Henri Clay Street, and next door where Tante Belle (also known as Nannan) lived is where my sister and her family now reside. The path through the connecting back yards is still much traveled.

The church square still dominates downtown, and I found some of the same old cracks in the sidewalk where we once lined up for school Mass. What used to be the old library, then Hebert's Cafe where we used to meet Mama and Papa for lunch, no longer emits the aromas of shrimp stew and lemon pie. At the next corner, next door to the old Teche Theater, used to be the soda fountain where my brother and I shared hot dogs, fountain cokes, and ice cream sundaes. The theater is closed and the aroma of freshly popped popcorn no longer wafts in the Saturday afternoon breeze.

The old convent where the nuns lived for nearly 100 years has been torn down, plank by plank, and now there is only the sidewalk leading up to the now-vacant lot. My old school, which in a previous life was once a hotel, is now a bed and breakfast, and now my first-grade classroom is a dining room. The old ice house and the nearby fish market have been demolished, and the sound of ice being crushed in the wicked-looking ice crusher that stood on the apron of the old building is no more. Also gone are the smells of fresh fish and other seafood that was packed on ice nearby at the fish market.

One day I stopped by a vacant lot where there once stood the old Fuselier Camp. I recalled the many gatherings we enjoyed there. There was always a crowd! Young children went wild on the lawn that dipped toward the bayou. Teenagers lounged on the small wharf, and adults sat on the porch in old theater seats that lined the walls. In the "Big Room" there was always a huge table laden with platters of pork roast, rice dressing, and desserts of all kinds.

Irene Fuselier was an accomplished hostess and often served what we called "morzette." I don't know how this dish came to be called by this name, nor do I know its origins, but I do know that it has everything but the kitchen sink in it.

It serves about 20, so it's ideal for parties.

Morzette

Makes 20 servings

3 pounds of lean ground beef
1 cup of chopped green bell peppers
½ cup of chopped yellow onions
2 cans (8 ounces each) of tomato sauce
4 packages (8 ounces each) of egg noodles
2 cans (4 ounces each) of chopped
   mushrooms with their juice
2 cans (16 ounces each) of whole-kernel
   corn, drained
1 jar (10 ounces) of salad olives,
   drained and chopped
3 cans (10 3/4 ounces each) of tomato soup
Garlic powder, salt, and cayenne, to taste
1 pound of bacon, fried and crumbled

Preheat the oven to 300 degrees.

Brown the meat in a large pot with the bell pepper and onions. Add the tomato sauce and allow the mixture to cook down for about 30 minutes.

In a separate pot, boil the noodles, drain, and add to the browned meat.

Add the mushrooms, corn, olives and two cans of the tomato soup, and mix well. Season with garlic powder, salt and cayenne.

Pour everything into a large baking dish. Mix the remaining can of soup with the crumbled bacon and spread over the top of the mixture.

Bake for one hour, covered. Uncover and bake for an additional 15 minutes.

Irene's brother, Stanley Stockstill, made some of the best pralines around.

Acadiana Pralines

Makes about 2 dozen

1 cup of sugar
½ cup of heavy cream
3 tablespoons of dark corn syrup
Pinch of baking soda
Pinch of salt
2 cups of pecan halves
½ teaspoon of pure vanilla extract

In a heavy 2-quart saucepan, combine the sugar, cream, corn syrup, baking soda and salt. Cook over medium heat, stirring a few times, until the sugar dissolves and the mixture comes to a boil. Continue boiling, without stirring, until the mixture reaches 234 degrees on a candy thermometer or forms a soft ball when a little of the mixture is dropped in cold water.

Remove from heat. Add the pecans and vanilla, stirring until creamy and the mixture covers the pecans with a slightly opaque coating.

Drop by the heaping teaspoon onto waxed paper and allow to cool completely before storing the pralines in an airtight container.

Cooking with our friends

Several times a year, Rock and I join two other couples, Ronnie (He and Rock have been friends since high school.) and his wife Kay, and Judy (She and I go back to college days.) and her husband Luke for a good visit, and of course, a meal of some kind.

I must tell you, Ronnie is a gourmet of the highest order. That man can cook anything, make it look easy, and, above all, make it taste divine! Since he knows a lot about wine, the meal he prepares is always accompanied by the finest spirits. You should also know that Ronnie is a gentleman, a great *raconteur*, and a *bon vivant*!

One evening we convened at his and Kay's home, a wonderful sprawling place that's ideal for entertaining. More often than not everyone hovers in the kitchen around a formidable waist-high chopping block. That's where we savored our glasses of champagne and nibbled on smoked salmon and fabulous caviar. Nothing is too good for Ronnie's friends!

As we imbibed, I noted that not a pot simmered on the stove, nor did a fire blaze in his great outdoor barbecue pit. I was curious about what grand meal was to be served.

Before I could comment, Ronnie and Kay announced that we were *all* going to participate in the preparation of our feast. A large bowl of fresh shrimp was pulled from the refrigerator. There followed another bowl containing several duck breasts Ronnie had procured from a hunting buddy. A basket of potatoes was brought forth from under the counter. A tray of spices and fresh herbs perched near the stove. Each couple

was to choose ingredients they wanted to prepare, as well as the method. We could do whatever we wanted with what was at hand. Rock grabbed the shrimp, Ronnie chose the duck breasts, and Luke ended up with the potatoes. Dessert was already taken care of: Ronnie had made several batches of his incredible chocolate chip cookies.

It was a wild and crazy evening, and the meal was fantastic!

Shrimp Remoulade

Makes 6 servings

1/2 cup of olive oil
1/4 cup of fresh lemon juice
1/4 cup of Creole mustard
1 tablespoon of mayonnaise
2 tablespoons of prepared horseradish
1/2 cup of minced celery
1/4 cup of minced fresh parsley
1/3 cup of minced onions
1 clove of garlic, minced
1 tablespoon of finely chopped green onions (green part only)
1 teaspoon of salt
2 teaspoons of sweet paprika
1/8 teaspoon of cayenne
3 dashes of Tabasco
2 pounds of cooked, peeled shrimp

In a blender or food processor, blend the olive oil, lemon juice, mustard, mayonnaise and horseradish for 20 seconds.

Pour this mixture into a mixing bowl and add the rest of the ingredients except for the shrimp. Mix well with a wooden spoon.

Pour into an airtight container and refrigerate.

When ready to use, toss the mixture with the shrimp and refrigerate until you are ready to serve.

Pan-Fried Duck Breasts

Makes 10 servings

20 boneless duck breasts
Salt, garlic powder, and coarsely ground
   black pepper, to taste
1½ cups of clarified butter

Rub the breasts generously with the dry seasonings. Pour about four tablespoons of clarified butter into a large, heavy skillet, heat the butter, and quickly fry three to four duck breasts, leaving them a bit rare. Pour off the butter and repeat the process until all of the breasts are cooked.

Keep the duck breasts warm in a covered dish in the oven.

I like to serve the breasts over wild rice to which I have added raisins and chopped pecans. A wonderful vegetable accompaniment to the duck breasts is a stir fry of julienne red bell pepper, zucchini, tiny fresh asparagus, and green beans flavored with butter and fresh basil.

Potatoes Anna

Makes 6 to 8 servings

6 medium Idaho potatoes, peeled
   and thinly sliced
1½ sticks of butter or margarine
Salt and freshly ground black pepper, to taste

Preheat the oven to 425 degrees.

Melt three tablespoons of the butter in a large black iron or other oven-proof skillet. Lay overlapping slices of potato all around the bottom of the skillet. Dot generously with butter and sprinkle lightly with salt and pepper. Continue to make layers in this way until all of the potato slices are used.

Cover the skillet and bake for 30 to 40 minutes or until the potatoes are tender. I usually bake this for five to eight minutes more, uncovered, to lightly brown the tops of the potatoes.

Now here is the trick: Take a warm, round serving platter a little larger than the skillet, place it on top of the potatoes, and quickly flip the skillet over so that the potato cake drops out.

Speaking of potatoes, they are not as popular as rice is in Louisiana, but we consume our fair share of them. They are usually teamed with meat, like steaks or baked brisket, but I feel that they go well with poultry and seafood as well.

Every so often I go on a potato craze. Sometimes I can't seem to pass the potato bins and displays in supermarkets without filling up a bag. I pick up sweet potatoes, Idahos, red (small and large) and those buttery Yukon Golds. Rock says I had best be careful because those potatoes are not only sticking to my ribs, but also to my hips and other parts of my body. But there are times when I indulge.

My brother Henri Clay (right) celebrates his first birthday in 1942 with a friend, Bobbie Thomas, who also celebrates her first.

Escalloped Potatoes

Makes 6 servings

6 medium-size red potatoes
1 teaspoon of salt
¼ teaspoon of cayenne
½ teaspoon of freshly ground black pepper
4 tablespoons of all-purpose flour
1 large yellow onion, thinly sliced
1 pint (maybe a little more) of milk
   or half-and-half
3 tablespoons of butter, cut into chips
4 tablespoons of grated, mild cheddar
   cheese

Preheat the oven to 350 degrees.

Peel the potatoes and cut crosswise into ¼-inch slices.

In a mixing bowl, combine the salt, cayenne pepper, black pepper and flour. Add the potato slices and toss to coat with the seasonings.

In a lightly buttered baking dish, layer the potatoes and onions, making two or three layers, until everything is used. Pour in the milk or half-and-half so that the liquid covers the potatoes. Dot with butter and bake for 45 minutes to an hour or until the potatoes are tender.

Sprinkle with grated cheese and serve.

Potato Casserole

Makes 8 to 10 servings

½ pound of bacon, chopped and crisply fried
10 Irish potatoes, boiled and peeled
1 cup of chopped onions
3 tablespoons of chopped green onions
   (green part only)
¾ pound of Velveeta or cheddar cheese,
   grated
½ cup of butter, melted
1 teaspoon of salt
½ teaspoon of cayenne
1 carton (16 ounce) of sour cream

Preheat the oven to 300 degrees.

In a large mixing bowl, combine the bacon and potatoes. Mash the potatoes well. Add the onions, cheese, butter, salt, cayenne and sour cream, and mix well.

Put the mixture into a lightly buttered baking pan large enough to accommodate the mixture. Bake for 30 minutes or until bubbly.

Potatoes with Garlic & Cheese

Makes 6 servings

6 Idaho potatoes, thinly sliced
1 tablespoon of chopped garlic
3 tablespoons of butter, melted
2 tablespoons of finely chopped chives or
   green onions (green part only)
2 tablespoons of grated Parmesan cheese
½ teaspoon of salt
¼ teaspoon of cayenne
¼ teaspoon of freshly ground black pepper

Preheat the oven to 350 degrees.

Put the potatoes in a large baking pan, arranging them evenly so that they just overlap each other. Sprinkle with garlic, melted butter, chives or green onions, cheese, salt, cayenne and black pepper.

Bake for 30 to 35 minutes, until lightly brown.

Oh, and while I'm at it, following is a recipe for baked brisket that's simple. If you have some left over, thinly sliced brisket is great on sandwiches spread with guacamole and sprinkled with chopped red onions. Yum!

My parents' 40th anniversary party in 1980 was well-attended by my nieces (their grandchildren). Front row, from left, are Becki Landry, Nicole Bienvenu, Suzanne Bienvenu and Monique Bienvenu. Back row: Catherine Bienvenu, Therese Bienvenu and Andrea Landry.

*My parents' 40th anniversary party in 1980 was graced by the
presence of my nephews (their grandsons). From left to right
are Ben Landry, Marti Bienvenu and Jeff Landry.*

Baked Brisket

Makes about 10 servings

¼ cup of soy sauce
¼ cup of vegetable or olive oil
1 tablespoon of coarsely ground
    black pepper
½ teaspoon of garlic powder
1½ cups of beer
One 5-pound fresh brisket, trimmed of fat

Preheat the oven to 450 degrees.

Combine all of the seasonings, place the brisket in a large dish or roasting pan, and pour the seasonings over the meat. Cover and marinate in the refrigerator for at least eight hours, turning the brisket two or three times during that period.

When you are ready to bake, put the brisket in the pan, fat side up, with the marinade. Brown the meat in the hot oven, reduce heat to 375 degrees, cover, and bake for two to three hours or until fork-tender.

Slice and serve with pan gravy.

But then again you might want to serve your potatoes with chicken.

Now, let me tell you about going shopping for chicken with Mama. She really inspects them. She pinches, presses, smells and prods those poor things before she selects the birds that come home with her. She wants them to be "nice, plump and pink." Those are her words, I swear. And look out if she notices a sale! She'll come home with several to store in the freezer.

"You never know when you'll need a chicken or two," she advises.

Here's one of her chicken dishes, cooked with onions, tomatoes and all kinds of good stuff.

Chicken Creole

Makes 4 to 6 servings

¼ cup of vegetable oil
1 fryer, about 3 pounds, cut into
    serving pieces
1 cup of chopped yellow onions
½ cup of chopped green bell peppers
2 tablespoons of all-purpose flour
1 (16-ounce) can of whole tomatoes
1 teaspoon of chopped garlic
2 bay leaves
Salt and cayenne, to taste
½ cup of dry white wine
2 (10½-ounce) cans of beef consommé
3 tablespoons of fresh parsley leaves

In a large heavy pot, heat the oil over medium-high heat. Add the chicken pieces and cook, browning the pieces evenly on all sides. Transfer the chicken to a platter and set aside.

Add the onions and bell peppers to the pot and reduce heat to medium. Cook, stirring, until they are soft, about five minutes. Add the flour and stir constantly for about five minutes. Add the tomatoes, garlic and bay leaves. With the back of a spoon, crush the tomatoes. Season with salt and cayenne. Cook for five minutes.

Add the wine and consommé. Cook for about 20 minutes, stirring occasionally.

Return the chicken to the pot, cover, and simmer for about 40 minutes or until the chicken is tender. Add the parsley and serve with steamed white long-grain rice.

Here is a dish I created with one of her nice, pink, plump birds. I sometimes get rather tired of boneless, skinless chicken breasts, and there's so much more flavor when using chicken on the bone.

Chicken with Shallots & Artichokes

Makes 4 to 6 servings

1 fryer, about 3 pounds, cut into
    serving pieces
6 tablespoons of butter
2 tablespoons of vegetable oil
16 peeled shallots
Salt and freshly ground black pepper,
    to taste
2 bay leaves
1 teaspoon of fresh lemon juice
1 (9-ounce) package of frozen artichoke
    hearts, defrosted and drained
½ cup of chicken broth

Rinse the chicken with cool water and pat dry with paper towels.

In a large, heavy skillet, preferably cast-iron, heat four tablespoons of the butter and the vegetable oil over medium-high heat. Brown the chicken, a few pieces at a time, starting with the skin side down. Turn the pieces to brown them evenly. Transfer the chicken to a platter.

Add the shallots to the skillet and cook, shaking the pan to color them lightly and evenly. Pour off all but a thin film of oil and return the chicken to the skillet. Season with salt and pepper. Lay the bay leaves on top of the chicken and cover the pot. Cook over high heat for about two minutes. Reduce the heat and simmer, uncovered. Baste with the pan juices.

In another skillet, heat the remaining two tablespoons of butter. Add the lemon juice and stir to combine. Add the artichoke hearts and season with a little salt. Cook over low heat for about 10 minutes or until the artichoke hearts are tender. After the chicken has cooked for about 30 minutes, test for doneness. If the chicken juices run clear, it is done.

Add the artichokes to the skillet with the chicken and the shallots, stir, and cook for five minutes. Remove and discard the bay leaves. Transfer the chicken, shallots and artichokes to a serving platter and keep warm.

Add the chicken broth to the pan juices and bring to a boil. Scrape any browned bits on the bottom of the pan and stir. Cook for two to three minutes and pour over the chicken. Serve immediately.

Pickin' pecans

I have another chicken recipe up my sleeve, but you'll have to endure a pecan story first.

One year the five-year-old next door (Her name is Taylor.) really got into picking "pah-corns," and every afternoon for about a week she banged on my door. One day she banged on my office door.

"Miss Marcelle, where's Rocko-Daddy? Can he come help me pick pah-corns? Mama says she'll bake us some cookies if we have some pah-corns!" Taylor said.

"Well, Tay, Rocko-Daddy is not back from work yet," I explained.

Her face showed utter disappointment and frustration.

I was tempted to give her a bag of my stash of shelled pecans from the freezer and send her on her way, but instead I offered to help her with her task.

She mulled that over for a few seconds and took me up on my offer. I guess somebody is better than nobody.

"Where would you like to go picking? Here in my yard or yours?" I questioned.

"My house. Our pah-corns are bigger than yours."

Smart kid!

For an hour, we scrambled on all fours, scooping up handsful at a time. When our bag was full, I called it quits. My knees were hurting and my back ached.

"I think we have enough now, Tay. But we'll have to crack and shell them before your mother can use them."

After about 20 minutes, we both lost interest. We made a deal. I gave her a bag of shelled pecans from my freezer in exchange for the bag we picked. Off she went, skipping through the yard. Rock didn't know it yet, but I had a project for him that night – to crack and shell those pah-corns.

He would be rewarded with a chicken and pecan dish as well as with some pecan cookies.

*   *   *

Keith Courrégé of New Iberia was a longtime friend of mine and Rock's, and, boy, could he cook! He was also a delightful gentleman.

The day I heard that he had passed away, my heart was heavy, but only for a minute. I chuckled as I thought what

fun the angels in heaven must be having, and how well they will be eating!

You see, Keith was the epitome of a *bon vivant* of the old school. With a smile forever on his face, he thought life was indeed a bowl of cherries and rarely did he get any pits. For most of his life, his avocation was cooking, and he graciously shared his creations with his friends, young and old.

The morning of his funeral service, I stole away to my office for a few moments of reminiscence. I found a little box with some of the recipes he had shared with me over the years. On top was the last note I received from him thanking me for a recipe. Of course, he mentioned that he was going to make it his own by adding a little of this and a little of that.

He adored entering cooking contests, and I had stashed in my files several newspaper clippings about some of his award-winning recipes. Just two years before he died, barely able to walk, he pitted his skills against about one hundred other aspiring non-professional cooks and walked away with a first place ribbon once again! When I gave him a congratulatory hug, he winked at me.

"See, I haven't lost my touch!" he said with a smile.

No, Keith, you never lost your touch.

His smoked brisket melted in your mouth and his crawfish creations were, well, heavenly!

I have in my possession a little book he did called *Pecans – From Soup To Nuts*, and I'm not embarrassed to say that I have snitched several recipes from it on many occasions.

The children of my niece, Therese Bienvenu Bennett, were getting ready for Halloween 2004 by donning their new Halloween headpieces. Left to right are Katy, Therese and Alyssa. Shane is on his mom's lap.

Here's the chicken dish I fixed for Rock with our bag of pecans.

Keith's Baked Pecan Chicken

Makes about 10 servings

1 cup of buttermilk
1 large egg, beaten
1 cup of all-purpose flour
1 cup of pecan meal (Grind the pecans to a fine meal in a food processor.)
½ cup of grated Parmesan cheese
1 tablespoon of sweet paprika
1 tablespoon of salt
Cayenne, to taste
2 broiler-fryer chickens (each about 2½ pounds), cut into serving pieces
1½ sticks of butter
¾ cup of pecan halves

Preheat the oven to 350 degrees.

Mix the buttermilk and egg in a mixing bowl. In another mixing bowl, combine the next six ingredients.

Dip the chicken pieces in the egg mixture and then it the flour-pecan mixture.

Melt the butter in a large, oblong baking dish. Place the chicken pieces in the baking dish, turning to coat with the butter, ending with the skin side up, and sprinkle with the pecan halves.

Bake for about an hour or until the chicken is nicely browned.

I also want to share with you Keith's recipe for *cassoulet*, a dish that's popular in the provinces of France, made with white beans and various meats. The classic *cassoulet* takes about three days to prepare and assemble, but Keith's version shortens the time up a bit. As he pointed out to me one day, this recipe is intended primarily for the cook who has a reasonable amount of culinary know-how.

Keith's *Cassoulet*

Makes 10 to 12 servings

Prepare in advance:
　　1 pound or 2 cups of dried Great Northern white beans, cooked with onions, garlic and salt pork, seasoned with green onions and parsley, and cooked until done, but not too thick

1 small domestic duck baked to a golden brown and cut into small serving pieces
½ pound of lean pork and ½ pound of lamb, cut into 1-inch chunks, sautéed in tomato and white wine gravy seasoned with onions, garlic, celery, bay leaves and thyme
½ pound of pork sausage (plain, smoked, or garlic-flavored), cooked and cut crosswise into ½-inch slices
¾ cup of Italian-style bread crumbs
4 tablespoons of duck fat or butter

Preheat the oven to 400 degrees.

Rub the inside of a deep 4- to 5-quart ovenproof casserole dish with a cut clove of garlic. Put a layer of beans in the bottom, then add a layer of mixed meats, then a layer of beans, a layer of meat, and end up with a layer of beans on top.

If there isn't enough liquid, add a little chicken broth. When adding the meat to the dish, be sure to include any gravy from the pans.

Spread the top with the bread crumbs and drizzle with the fat or butter.

Heat the casserole on top of the stove until it begins to bubble, and transfer it to the oven and bake, uncovered, for 15 to 20 minutes, or until a crust forms on the top. Push the crust down into the dish, reduce the heat to 350 degrees, and continue to bake until another crust forms. Push it down into the dish. This can be repeated two or three times and baked for a total of about one hour. Add a little broth if the mixture becomes dry. Leave the final crust intact for serving.

Cookin' with leeks

One year a gentleman presented me with some leeks from his garden. I planted them according to his directions in a well-drained garden loam, fertilized the soil, and applied an organic mulch during the winter months. And then I waited. Nothing much happened during the spring and summer, and I assumed I had done them in.

Then one fall as I was working my flower beds, I spied several shoots springing from the earth. Lo and behold, my leeks were coming up!

I had not paid much attention to leeks in the produce section of my supermarket until the last couple of years, and now I am infatuated with them. Rock calls them big overgrown green onions. But he's learned that although they are similar to green onions, they are milder in flavor and more versatile.

I now have a collection of several luscious recipes. The first one, I must confess, comes from my friend Hallman Woods, a fastidious cook, who with his wife and son operated a jewel of a restaurant (and a bed and breakfast) called *Le Rosier* in New Iberia, La. Here's to you, Big Hallman!

When selecting leeks, choose those with crisp, brightly colored leaves. When preparing them, trim off the root and leaf ends, then cut them lengthwise

All my nieces were cute kids, including Therese and Catherine Bienvenu, shown in this 1973 photo. Pictured above is Catherine 20 years later.

and wash thoroughly to remove all the dirt trapped between the leaves.

I should also explain to you what tasso is. It's heavily spiced smoked pork, and if you can't find it in your super-market, you can substitute lean bacon or smoked ham.

Cream of Leek Soup with Tasso

Makes 6 to 8 servings

1 stick (8 tablespoons) of butter
½ cup plus 1 tablespoon of all-purpose flour
2 to 3 cups of coarsely chopped leeks, white and green parts
1 cup of finely chopped tasso
2 quarts of chicken stock
6 ounces of heavy cream
Salt, freshly ground black pepper, and Tabasco, to taste

First, make the roux. The roux, consisting of the flour and butter, must cook over a moderate heat with bubbling present for three to four minutes, or otherwise there will be an uncooked flour taste. The roux should be watched and stirred so that it does not brown and remains the color of the butter.

Into the hot roux, add the leeks and tasso, and cook for two to three minutes. While stirring slowly, add the stock and simmer for 10 minutes, or until the leeks are as tender as you like. Add the heavy cream and return to a simmer for another two to three minutes, then season to taste.

The next recipe is my creation. I suggest using Italian plum tomatoes for this.

Marcelle's Leeks & Tomatoes

Makes 4 to 6 servings

3 leeks, washed, split lengthwise, and
    chopped into 1-inch pieces
2 cups of chicken broth
¼ teaspoon of freshly ground black pepper
6 Italian plum tomatoes, sliced
1 tablespoon of olive oil
1 teaspoon of balsamic vinegar

Place the leeks and broth in a saucepan, bring to a boil, and then turn off the heat and let the leeks sit for three minutes. Drain off about half of the broth and place the leeks and the remaining broth in a deep bowl.

Add the black pepper and the tomatoes, and toss with the olive oil and vinegar.

Cool the salad in the refrigerator for 15 minutes before serving.

I'm on a roll. Here are two more leek recipes.

Duck with Leeks in Mustard Sauce

Makes 2 servings

4 tablespoons of butter
1 large leek (white part only), rinsed in cool
    water and thinly sliced
2 boneless duck (or chicken) breasts, about
    4 to 5 ounces each
6 tablespoons of dry vermouth
6 tablespoons of dry white wine
¼ cup plus 2 tablespoons of heavy cream
1 tablespoon of coarse-grained mustard
Salt and freshly ground black pepper,
    to taste

Melt two tablespoons of the butter in a heavy skillet over medium-low heat. Add the leek and cook until tender, stirring occasionally, about five minutes. Remove from the heat and set aside.

Melt the remaining two tablespoons of butter in another skillet over medium-high heat. Add the duck or chicken breasts and cook for three to four minutes on each side for the duck (five to six minutes on each side of the chicken). Transfer the breasts to a heated plate. Tent a piece of foil over the breasts to keep warm.

Add the vermouth to the same skillet and increase heat to medium-high to bring to a boil, scraping any brown bits in the skillet. Add the wine and boil until the liquid is reduced by half, about four minutes. Add the cream and boil until reduced by half, about three minutes. Whisk in the mustard. Season with salt and pepper.

Add the reserved leeks to the sauce and serve over the duck or chicken breasts.

Baked Rice with Leeks

Makes 6 servings

4 large leeks, about 2½ pounds
6 tablespoons of butter
1/2 teaspoon of salt
1/4 teaspoon of freshly ground black pepper
3 cups of cooked long-grain white rice
1/2 cup of grated sharp cheddar cheese
2 large eggs
3/4 cup of heavy cream
1/4 cup plus 2 tablespoons of milk
1/4 teaspoon of grated nutmeg
1/4 teaspoon of salt
1/8 teaspoon of cayenne

Preheat the oven to 350 degrees.

Trim the leeks leaving three inches of green. Cut them cross-wise into half-inch slices. Rinse the leeks thoroughly, drain and pat dry.

Melt five tablespoons of the butter in a saucepan over low heat. Add the leeks, salt and black pepper. Cover and cook until the leeks are tender, 15 to 20 minutes. Stir in the rice and half of the cheese.

Generously butter a 2-quart baking dish. Beat the eggs, cream, milk, nutmeg, salt and pepper in a large bowl. Add the rice and leek mixture and toss well. Spoon into the baking dish, spreading evenly.

Cover and bake for 15 minutes. Sprinkle with remaining cheese and dot with the remaining butter. Bake uncovered until the cheese is melted and lightly browned, about 5 to 10 minutes.

Hot soups for the Cajun soul

When the weather is dark, gray and chilly, you can bet your last dollar that my sister Edna has a pot of soup simmering on the stove. She claims it makes her large kitchen feel warm and cozy. A friend of mine says making a *potage* is therapeutic when she's had a bad day or is down in the dumps. Rock is a super souper and is perfectly happy having soup at any meal, especially when it's cold outside.

I agree, soup is definitely one of those comfort foods that makes people feel good. I like salads with soups, and an old-time favorite is this one that Papa used to enjoy.

Chilled Beet Salad

Makes about 6 servings

1 medium red onion, thinly sliced
1 (16-ounce) can of sliced beets, drained
2 tablespoons of olive oil
2 tablespoons of apple cider vinegar
Pinch of sugar
1 tablespoon of sour cream
Salt and freshly ground black pepper,
    to taste
2 cups of butter lettuce, washed and torn
    into bite-sized pieces

Chill the onion and beets in a covered bowl for two hours.

Whisk together the olive oil, vinegar, sugar, sour cream, pepper and salt. Toss with the onions, beets and butter lettuce to serve.

These are some of the soups that keep the body and soul warm and happy.

Eggplant Soup

Makes 6 to 8 servings

¼ cup of vegetable oil
3 medium eggplants, peeled and cubed
1½ cups of chopped yellow onions
½ cup of chopped celery
1 cup of chopped tomatoes, fresh or canned
2 quarts of chicken broth
3 cups of cooked and cubed chicken (or 3 cups of peeled and deveined raw shrimp)
Salt and cayenne, to taste
Pinch of dried thyme leaves

Heat the oil in a medium-size saucepan over medium heat. Add the eggplant, onions and celery, and cook, stirring, until they are soft, about 10 to 12 minutes.

Add the tomatoes and cook for 20 minutes, stirring often. Add a little of the chicken broth if the mixture sticks to the bottom of the pot.

Add the broth and stir to mix well. Reduce the heat to medium-low and simmer for 30 minutes.

Add the chicken or shrimp, season with salt and cayenne, and add the thyme. Simmer for 20 minutes. Serve immediately.

My great-nephew Shane Bennett gives Papa Rock a kiss in the fall of 2004.

Andouille & Black Bean Soup

Makes 6 servings

¼ cup of vegetable oil
1 pound of andouille, cut cross-wise into ¼-inch slices
2 teaspoons of chopped garlic
2 cups of chopped yellow onions
½ cup of chopped celery
3 cups of dried black beans
2½ cups of chicken broth
¼ cup of chopped fresh parsley leaves
1 teaspoon of dried oregano leaves
2 pinches of ground cumin
½ teaspoon of salt (more or less, to taste)
¼ teaspoon of freshly ground black pepper
Tabasco, to taste
Sour cream, chopped green onions, and chopped fresh cilantro leaves for garnish

In a large saucepan, heat the oil over medium heat and brown the andouille for about five minutes. Add the garlic, onions and celery, and cook, stirring, for two to three minutes. Add the black beans, chicken broth, parsley, cumin and oregano, and bring to a boil. Reduce the heat, cover, and simmer for two hours or until the beans are tender. If the mixture becomes too thick during the cooking time, add more broth.

Add the salt, black pepper and Tabasco after the soup has simmered for two hours. If you want a creamier or smoother soup, puree half of the mixture in a food processor and return to the pot, or you can mash some of the beans against the side of the pot with the back of a wooden spoon.

To serve, garnish the bowls of soup with the sour cream, green onions and cilantro.

My great-nieces are all-smiles in May of 2001. Left to right: Alyssa and Katy Bennett, and Madison and Hannah Alford.

To go along with your black bean soup, try a salad of assorted mixed greens tossed with this dressing.

Avocado Dressing

Makes about 1 cup

1 ripe avocado, about 8 to 10 ounces
2 tablespoons of fresh lime juice
2 tablespoons of virgin olive oil
¼ teaspoon of coarsely ground black pepper
Salt, to taste
1 teaspoon of minced pimientos
2 medium garlic cloves, minced
1 tablespoon of minced red onions

Halve the avocado, remove the pit, and scoop the flesh into a small mixing bowl. Add the lime juice and mash together with a fork. Add the olive oil and incorporate it into the mixture. Add the black pepper, salt, pimientos, garlic and onions, and mix well. If you want a smoother dressing, you can puree it in a food processor until smooth. Chill for at least an hour before serving.

Apple desserts

Simple desserts go well with soup and salad meals, and just about anything made with apples is a winner in my book.

I remember one occasion when somehow my grocery cart bumped into an apple display as I turned the corner in the produce department at the supermarket. There were apples rolling everywhere – Granny Smith, Gala, Macintosh, Delicious – skidding down the cereal aisle, headed for the flower department, some causing customers to jump like football players going through a workout.

A nearby stock boy rolled his eyes while a voice came over the loudspeaker asking for assistance in the produce department. My first thought was to abandon my cart and make a mad dash for the door, never again to return. Then I decided to humbly apologize to anyone within earshot and got down on my hands and knees to help gather up the red, yellow and green fruit that seemed to have multiplied as it fell.

The store manager appeared at my side in a minute and assured me that it was unnecessary for me to help clean up the mess. I think he just wanted me away from the area as quickly as possible. As I sheepishly went down the baking goods aisle I noticed that a dozen or so of the apples had landed in my cart. Oh, well, I needed apples anyway and they would make great desserts.

Apple Fritters

Makes 4 to 6 servings

2 tart apples, peeled, cored, and sliced into 1/4-inch rings
1 tablespoon of brandy
2 teaspoons of fresh lemon juice
1 large egg
1 tablespoon of sugar
½ teaspoon of grated lemon zest
¼ cup of room-temperature buttermilk
½ tablespoon of butter, melted
½ cup of all-purpose flour
½ teaspoon of baking soda
¼ teaspoon of salt
Oil for frying
Powdered sugar for dusting

In a large bowl, toss the apples with half of the brandy and the lemon juice and let stand for an hour at room temperature.

For the batter, whisk the egg, sugar and lemon zest in a small mixing bowl until it is light in color and forms a ribbon when trailed from the whisk. Beat in the remaining brandy, the buttermilk and the butter. Sift the flour with the baking soda and salt and fold into the buttermilk mixture. If the batter is too thick, add one or two more teaspoons of buttermilk.

Heat about two inches of oil to 360 degrees in a deep fryer or frying pan. Drain the apple slices and pat dry. Dip the apple slices, one or two at a time, into the batter to coat evenly, letting the excess batter drip off.

Fry the apple slices in hot oil until the bottom of each slice is golden brown and the coating has puffed. Carefully turn the slices and fry until golden brown. Drain on paper towels and dust with powdered sugar.

Honey Baked Apples

Makes 5 servings

5 large baking apples
3 tablespoons of chopped pecans
3 tablespoons of raisins
1 cup of water
1/3 cup of honey
2 teaspoons of ground cinnamon
1 tablespoon of fresh lemon juice

Preheat the oven to 350 degrees.

Core the apples, peeling the top third of each. Place the apples in a shallow baking dish. Combine the pecans and raisins and stuff the cavities of the apples with this mixture.

Combine the water, honey and cinnamon in a small saucepan and bring to a boil. Reduce the heat and simmer for five minutes. Remove from the heat, add the lemon juice, and pour the liquid over the apples.

Cover and bake for 45 to 50 minutes, basting occasionally, until the apples are tender.

St. Martinville's Pepper Fest

As you may or may not know, Louisianians love to honor and celebrate just about anything, and they do this by having festivals. On most autumn weekends, you can find a festival celebrating anything from local crops, like rice, sugarcane, yams, strawberries and watermelons, to animals, like frogs, crawfish, pigs and shrimp, as well as the cultural arts.

In my hometown of St. Martinville we celebrate with a Pepper Fest. Shop owners decorate their store fronts with pepper flags and garlands of dried peppers. The citizens sport pepper scarves around their necks, pepper earrings dangle from ear lobes, and local bands jam throughout the day making the town hot, hot, hot.

There's a pepper-eating contest during which contestants huff, puff and sweat. Food booths offer pepper-flavored jams, jellies and hot sauces. And, of course, there's a cooking contest featuring peppers.

My contribution is a cooking demonstration using local peppers.

Stuffed Banana Peppers

Makes 6 appetizer servings

12 fresh or pickled sweet banana peppers
2 packages (6 ounces) of softened
   cream cheese
¼ cup of cheese, such as crumbled
   Roquefort, grated sharp cheddar, or grated
   Monterey Jack
Tabasco, to taste
1 tablespoon of mayonnaise or sour cream
1 teaspoon of minced yellow onions
1 teaspoon of minced garlic
Sweet paprika

Wash and split the peppers in half lengthwise. Remove the seeds and veins. (If you are using fresh peppers, wear rubber gloves.)

Blend the remaining ingredients, except for the paprika, in a food processor or blender. Fill the pepper halves with the mixture and sprinkle with paprika.

The stuffed peppers may be served cold but may also be run under a broiler for a few minutes.

Sweet Red Bell Pepper Soup

Makes 6 servings

4 medium-size red bell peppers
2 tablespoons of butter
2 tablespoons of olive oil
2 cups of chicken broth
1 quart of heavy cream
Salt, cayenne, and Tabasco, to taste
1 pound of lump crabmeat, picked over
   for shells and cartilage

Split the peppers in half, remove the seeds and coarsely chop.

Heat the butter and olive oil in a large saucepan over medium heat. Add the peppers and cook, stirring, for two to three minutes, or until soft. Add the chicken broth and cook for five minutes.

Pour the mixture into a blender or food processor and process for 15 seconds.

Return the mixture to the pot. Add the cream, bring to a gentle boil, and reduce the mixture until it thickens slightly. Season with salt, cayenne and hot sauce. Add the crabmeat, reduce the heat, and simmer for five minutes. Serve immediately.

Tante May Judice Hains (left) and her sister, Belle "Nannan" Judice, are decked out in their Sunday best and ready to go to Christmas Mass around 1960. They were ideal stand-ins for the grandmothers we never knew; our grandmas died before I was born.

WINTER

Winter is not Louisiana's prettiest season. Most of the trees – cypress, pecan and oak – are bare, and we have little or no hope for snow to cling to the naked branches or to provide cold-weather activities. But that doesn't stop the locals from enjoying good times.

Truth be told, it's a special time for gathering with friends and relatives. One of the preferred pastimes is spending the day putting together a gumbo made with chicken and sausage, or seafood and okra, and letting it simmer for several hours while enjoying a game of *bourré* or watching football games on television.

The weeks that follow Thanksgiving are a festive time as families anticipate the Christmas holidays. There are dishes to be prepared in advance for the celebration tables and gifts to be made for exchanging.

Cher, it's cold outside, but it is warm and cozy in our homes and in our hearts.

Recalling the good ol' days

Can it be that my nieces and nephews are growing up? Those sweet little cherubs that I cuddled and spoiled are now young adults. Not having children of my own, they are very special to me, and I adore it when I hear them call me "Nani-Celle."

Not too long ago when they were all home the week before Christmas I had most of them over for dinner. The initial idea was to get a stash of dips and chips, and maybe make a pot of spaghetti, but one of the older girls suggested that we have a real sit-down dinner, complete with good china, silver and crystal. She even offered to plan the menu and help me cook.

"After all, Nani-Celle, we're big people now," she laughed.

While I put the finishing touches on the meal, I could hear them talking about some of their memories.

Remember when Ben drove his father's brand new riding lawn mower into the deep end of the swimming pool, and no one fussed at him? Everyone laughed for a long time, even when it was deemed necessary to hire men and equipment to lift the mower out.

And what about the time Pop-Pop's leg caught on fire at the camp? Thank goodness he had a prosthesis and no harm was done other than a new leg had to be purchased. Then there was the time prim and proper Uncle Jack fell out of the hammock and rolled down the bank into the lake.

Becki giggled as she recalled the time, shortly after getting her driver's license, when she tried to back out of the driveway and smashed into the locked wrought iron gate. But it was the four daughters of my brother Henri and his wife Maria who brought forth gales of laughter as they relived many incidents from their teenage years.

Then Jeff, a true *raconteur* who I predict one day will be either the governor of the state or maybe even the president of the United States, made us all double over in laughter when he recounted some of his mother's cooking experiences. My sister Edna is not much of a cook, but I have to say there is always food on the table at mealtime. Most of what she cooks has the addition of some kind of cream-of-something soup in it, and for ever so long Jeff thought perhaps they had stock in the Campbell soup company!

It was late when I tinkled the dinner bell, but the kids were ravenous and there wasn't a crumb left after it was all said and done.

Along with a pork loin, we enjoyed mashed potatoes tweaked with dill, butter and cream. Dessert was simple: hot coffee and homemade cookies.

Our immediate family was all together at Mama and Daddy's house for Christmas 1971, as usual. Seated, from left to right, are my sister Edna, Mama, Daddy and me. Behind us are brothers Bruce and Henri Clay.

Stuffed Pork Loin

Makes 6 to 8 servings

1½ to 2 pounds of boneless, trimmed pork tenderloin
2 tablespoons of soy sauce
½ teaspoon of freshly ground black pepper
½ teaspoon of garlic powder
1 tablespoon of olive oil
1 pound of sweet Italian sausage, removed from the casing and crumbled
1 cup of finely chopped green onions
½ cup of chopped pecans
¼ cup of raisins

Rub the pork tender with the soy sauce and dry seasonings and allow to marinate for one hour in the refrigerator. With a sharp boning knife, make a slit down the length of the pork tender large enough to hold the stuffing.

Preheat the oven to 425 degrees.

Cook the sausage in the olive oil in a heavy skillet over medium heat until all pink disappears. Add the green onions, pecans and raisins, and stir to mix. Remove from heat and allow the mixture to cool completely.

Press the stuffing into the cavity of the pork tender. Secure the stuffing with small skewers, toothpicks or kitchen twine. Place the tender in a shallow roasting pan and pour any marinade left in the pan over the meat.

Roast for 30 to 40 minutes, adding a little beef broth or water to the pan if it becomes dry. Do not overcook.

Remove the meat from the oven and remove the skewers, toothpick or twine. Let the meat rest for a couple of minutes before slicing across the grain into half-inch pieces.

Spoon the pan drippings over the meat to serve.

During the cold winter months, when there's a siege of rainy, foggy, dreary days, nothing takes the chill off better than a wild duck dinner accompanied by hearty vegetables.

Fortunately for me, my neighbor Butch shares his limit of mallards that I stash in the freezer for just such an occasion. I like to slow-bake my mallards for the better part of an afternoon. The vegetables can be prepared near serving time.

Although fresh limas are not available during the winter, I find that canned beans do just fine for this casserole.

Lima Bean Casserole

Makes 6 to 8 servings

2 tablespoons of vegetable oil
1 cup of chopped yellow onions
1 teaspoon of chopped garlic
3 (15-ounce) cans of baby lima beans, drained, with liquid reserved
1 tablespoon of cornstarch
1 cup of chopped black olives
2 tablespoons of chili powder
1 cup of grated cheddar cheese
Salt and white pepper, to taste

Preheat the oven to 350 degrees.

Heat the oil in a large skillet over medium heat. Add the onions and garlic and cook, stirring, for two to three minutes.

Dissolve the cornstarch in the reserved bean liquid and add to the skillet along with the chopped olives and chili powder.

Add the lima beans and one-half cup of the cheese and cook for five minutes, stirring until the cheese melts. Season with salt and white pepper.

Pour the mixture into a casserole and top with remaining cheese. Bake uncovered until the cheese bubbles, about 30 minutes.

Jerusalem artichokes, also called sunchokes, are not truly artichokes but a variety of sunflower with a lumpy, brown-skinned tuber that often resembles gingerroot. The name of this vegetable has nothing to do with Jerusalem but is derived from the Italian word for sunflower, *girasole*. They are usually available from October to March; the flesh is nutty, sweet and crunchy, and is ideal, I think, to serve with wild ducks. If you can't find them, substitute turnips.

Jerusalem Artichoke Casserole

Makes 6 servings

20 ounces of fresh Jerusalem artichokes
4 cups of water
2 teaspoons of fresh lemon juice
2 (6-ounce) packages of cream cheese, softened
¼ cup of butter
¼ cup plus 1 tablespoon of Parmesan cheese
Salt and cayenne, to taste
½ cup of cooking liquid
Paprika

Wash the artichokes in cool water. Place them in a deep saucepan and cover with water. Bring to a gentle boil over medium heat and cook until they are fork-tender. Drain, reserving the cooking liquid. Sprinkle the artichokes with the lemon juice, and cool.

Peel the artichokes and either slice or cube them. Arrange the pieces in a lightly buttered casserole dish.

Blend together the cream cheese, butter, one-fourth cup of the Parmesan cheese, and season with salt and pepper. Stir the mixture together with one-half cup of hot cooking liquid and pour over the artichokes. Sprinkle the casserole with the rest of the Parmesan cheese and the paprika.

Broil the casserole for three to four minutes or until slightly browned.

A hankering for oysters

Another wintertime tradition in south Louisiana is slurping down cold, plump oysters – those luscious mollusks harvested along the coastline of the Gulf of Mexico.

Oysters on the half-shell and fried oysters are popular for Friday night suppers in the predominantly Catholic communities of the state. It's nothing to find families, with grandparents and children in tow, queuing up at local oyster houses – like Black's, Dupuy's and Shuck's, in the quaint, historic town of Abbeville, in Vermilion Parish – on blustery winter evenings anxious to chomp down on a variety of oyster-based dishes.

In New Orleans, where the inhabitants believe oysters have aphrodisiac qualities, you're likely to see bumper stickers that read "Eat Louisiana oysters and love longer" – which is certainly a reason to consume your fair share. Here, oyster bars are crowded with well-dressed society matrons, truck drivers and businessmen standing elbow to elbow, throwing back a dozen or two raw oysters. The oysters are sometimes dipped in a ketchup sauce spiked liberally with horseradish and hot sauce, or at other times drizzled with nothing more than fresh lemon juice.

I remember one winter when I couldn't get enough oysters. The saga began one cool November day when I was in New Orleans on business. Before I left the city I lunched with several friends and sucked down six salty ones at the Acme Oyster House on the fringe of the French Quarter. I followed that up with another half dozen, fried.

On the way home, via Hwy. 90, I had a hankering for more. As I approached my turnoff at Hwy. 14 near New Iberia, I couldn't stand it. I pulled into a filling station and headed for the phone booth just as a thunderstorm moved in from the west.

"Rocky, how would you like to partake of some oysters?"

"Marcie B., you must have read my mind. Where are you?"

We agreed to meet in Abbeville in 30 minutes. The rain was coming down in torrents when we made our rendezvous. It seemed that half the population of Acadiana had the same idea, because our favorite oyster bar was filled to capacity.

While we waited for a table, we each enjoyed a dozen on the half shell, taken at the crowded bar. At the table we chowed down on fried oysters and went on to an old favorite, Oysters Bordelaise.

Oysters Bordelaise

Makes 4 appetizer or 2 main-course servings

6 tablespoons of butter
1 tablespoon of olive oil
1 tablespoon of minced garlic
1 tablespoon of minced green onions
1 tablespoon of flat-leaf parsley
1 teaspoon of Worcestershire sauce
¼ teaspoon of Tabasco
2 dozen freshly shucked oysters, drained
Salt, to taste
Fresh lemon juice, to taste

In a small saucepan, heat the butter and olive oil over medium heat. Add the garlic, green onions, parsley, Worcestershire sauce and Tabasco; cook for two to three minutes.

Place the oysters in a shallow roasting pan and pour the butter mixture over them. If your oysters are salty, forego the salt. Sprinkle with lemon juice and place the pan under the oven broiler for two to three minutes or until the edges of the oysters curl. Serve immediately.

Chicken & Oyster Pie

Makes 4 to 6 servings

3 heaping tablespoons of all-purpose flour
1 stick (½ cup) of butter
1 cup of chopped green onions
1/4 cup of chopped celery
1/2 cup of chopped fresh parsley leaves
2 whole chicken breasts, deboned, skinned, cooked, and cut into bite-sized pieces
2½ dozen oysters, drained, oyster liquor reserved
1/8 teaspoon of Tabasco
Pinch of thyme
1 bay leaf
1 (10-count) can of refrigerator biscuits

Preheat oven to 400 degrees.

On medium heat, cook the flour with the butter, stirring constantly, until the roux turns a rich, deep brown.

Add the green onions, celery and parsley, and cook, stirring, until the vegetables are limp, about three minutes,

Add the chicken and the oysters and season with salt, cayenne and Tabasco. Add the thyme and bay leaf, and cook until the edges of the oysters curl. Add the oyster liquor and stir until the sauce thickens. If the gravy becomes too thick, add a little chicken broth to thin it. Gently simmer until the mixture is bubbly hot. Remove and discard the bay leaf.

Pour into a 2-quart casserole and top with the biscuits. Bake until the biscuits are puffed and nicely browned, about 15 to 20 minutes.

My great aunts, Aunt "T" and Tante Tacia, were great cooks, and they also knew a thing or two about oyster pies. I've combined Mr. Keith's recipe and theirs for this pork and oyster pie. You may want to dabble with this one to make it your own. Mama says she doesn't use garlic, and Aunt Lois doesn't like bell peppers, so experiment to see what pleases your taste buds.

Pork & Oyster Pie

Makes 6 servings

2 (9-inch) pie crusts
¼ cup of vegetable oil
¼ cup of all-purpose flour
1 pound of lean ground beef
½ pound of lean ground pork
1 cup of minced yellow onions
½ cup of minced celery
½ cup of minced bell peppers
1 teaspoon of minced garlic
¼ cup of chopped green onions
1 tablespoon of minced fresh parsley leaves
2 dozen freshly shucked oysters, drained with liquor reserved
Salt and cayenne, to taste

Preheat the oven to 375 degrees. Bake one of the pie crusts until it is lightly golden. Remove it from the oven and let it cool completely.

Combine the oil and flour in a large, heavy skillet over medium heat. Stirring slowly and constantly, make a dark brown roux.

In another large skillet, cook the beef and pork until all of the pink disappears. Add the onions, celery, bell peppers, garlic, green onions and parsley and cook until the vegetables are soft, about five minutes. Drain off any excess oil. Add the roux and some of the oyster liquor if the mixture is too thick. The consistency should be like a thick stew.

Add the oysters. (You may want to chop the oysters; this is a matter of taste.) Season with salt and cayenne and pour into the baked pie shell.

Top the filling with the second crust, crimp the edges, and make several slashes on the top pie crust to vent steam while the pie is baking.

Bake until the crust is golden brown, 35 to 40 minutes.

There is no limit to what can be done with oysters, and these next two recipes are both divine.

A *croquette* is an old Acadiana favorite composed of minced meats or seafood (oysters, in this case) and seasonings, bound together with cream and cracker crumbs, and then formed into patties that are dipped in beaten egg and cracker crumbs or bread crumbs, and then deep-fried. They're great for appetizers.

Oyster *Croquettes*

Makes 4 to 6 servings

3 tablespoons of butter
2 dozen oysters, drained and chopped
2 tablespoons of chopped fresh
    parsley leaves
½ cup of cream or half-and-half
Salt and cayenne, to taste
Cracker crumbs for dredging
Vegetable oil for frying
1 large egg, beaten

Melt the butter in a saucepan over medium heat and add the chopped oysters and parsley. Cook, stirring, for one minute over medium heat, gradually adding the cream or half-and-half, stirring constantly. Season with salt and cayenne.

Remove the oyster mixture from the heat and add enough cracker crumbs to bind the mixture together. Allow the oysters to cool a bit and form into croquettes or small patties.

In a heavy pot or an electric fryer, heat four inches of oil to 360 degrees. Dip the patties in the beaten egg and then in the cracker crumbs. Drop two to three croquettes at a time into hot oil and deep-fry until they pop to the surface and are golden brown.

Drain on paper towels and serve.

Stuffed oysters are really not stuffed but combined with sausage and bread crumbs and then baked in cleaned oyster shells. If oyster shells are not available, the mixture can be cooked in a large casserole dish or in individual ramekins.

Stuffed Oysters

Makes 4 appetizer portions (3 each)

12 oyster shells
1 pound of country-style breakfast sausage
    or Italian sausage, removed from the
    casing and crumbled
1 pint of oysters, drained and chopped,
    liquor reserved
½ cup of minced fresh parsley leaves
½ cup of chopped green onions
4 hamburger or hot dog buns, dried in the
    oven and crumbled
¼ stick of butter or margarine
1½ tablespoons of fresh lemon juice
½ cup of Italian-style bread crumbs

Preheat the oven to 350 degrees.

Scrub the oyster shells in hot, soapy water, rinse, and boil to completely clean them. Drain and set aside.

Cook the sausage in a skillet over medium heat until all of the pink disappears. Add the oysters, parsley and green onions. Cook, stirring, for three minutes.

Mix-in the crumbled bread, the butter or margarine, and lemon juice. If the stuffing is too dry, add a little of the reserved oyster liquor. Blend well.

Spoon the oyster mixture, in equal portions, in the oyster shells (or place in ramekins or in a casserole dish) and top with the bread crumbs.

Bake until lightly golden and bubbly, 20 to 25 minutes.

The goodness of fresh tuna

While I'm on the subject of some of the best seafood Louisiana has to offer, I have to tell you about my introduction to fresh tuna. Like many people of a certain age, I didn't know there was anything but canned tuna out there because I never lived in an area where fresh tuna was readily available. However, in recent years there has been a great deal of interest in Louisiana for the yellowfin tuna caught in the deep waters of the Gulf of Mexico.

My introduction to fresh tuna happened on a deep-sea fishing trip in the Gulf aboard "The Sundown" with my friends Babs and Richard Grant. It was a ladies' fishing rodeo, and the first day out Babs hooked a big tuna. She and the fish fought like heck for several hours before the beautiful creature was brought aboard. It didn't win Babs a trophy, but it certainly provided us with a feast that evening, which we shared with the rest of the sport fishermen at the quaint marina down near the mouth of the Mighty Mississippi.

The meat of the yellowfin tuna is moist and bright pink, and Richard knew just how to cut it into steaks that didn't need much but a smattering of salt and pepper, a squeeze of lemon juice, and a rubbing of oil before we slapped them on the grill. It's best to cook the tuna to rare or medium rare, or else it will be dry. Don't be squeamish. After you taste it, you'll understand.

But of course, there's more than one way to prepare tuna. Let me tell you another tuna story.

One evening after work, I stopped at one of my favorite haunts called Joey's, an upscale Lafayette market that features top-of-the-line meats and seafood, fine domestic and imported cheeses, great wines and all sorts of goodies. I'm always an easy mark for the owner who is, of course, Joey.

"Hey, Marcelle," he greeted me with a wave from behind the counter. "How about some fresh tuna steaks. They just came in."

I had my mouth set for one of his thick-cut veal chops, but I told him to cut two tuna steaks while I selected a nice chardonnay, a wedge of brie cheese, and a loaf of fresh-baked whole-wheat French bread.

On the way home, I stopped at the corner grocery and picked out a pretty decent eggplant and a large red onion.

As I unpacked my treasures at home, I heard voices coming from my patio. I slid open the glass doors and found two of my neighbors comfortably settled in lounge chairs. On cue, they looked up and asked, "What's for supper?" At least they had brought along a couple of bottles of wine and a still-warm apple pie.

It was a case of the loaves and fishes. I thought quickly. The vegetables could be stretched, and I just would have to cut the thick tuna steaks in two to make four. I had planned to grill the fish, but I remember my friend Richard's success with panéed (breaded) tuna. Once more, I must tell you not to overcook the tuna.

My great-nieces, Madison and Hannah Alford, enjoy themselves while visiting at my house in 1996.

Panéed Tuna

Makes 4 servings

4 tuna steaks, about 1 inch thick
  (about 6 ounces each)
Salt, freshly ground black pepper,
  and cayenne, to taste
2 large eggs
¼ cup of Parmesan cheese
1½ cups of Italian-style bread crumbs
½ cup of clarified butter
2 tablespoons of olive oil

Pound the tuna between two sheets of wax paper to flatten the steaks out just a bit. Season with salt, black pepper and cayenne.

Beat the eggs well and add the Parmesan cheese. Dip the tuna in the egg mixture and then evenly coat with bread crumbs.

Sauté the tuna quickly in clarified butter and olive oil until lightly browned on both sides, turning once. Serve warm.

Broiled Eggplant & Red Onion

1 large eggplant, cut crosswise into
  ½-inch slices
1 large red onion, skinned and cut crosswise
  into ½-inch slices
Olive oil
Salt, freshly ground black pepper, and garlic
  powder, to taste

Rub the eggplant and onion slices with olive oil and season with salt, black pepper and garlic powder.

Place on an oiled broiler pan and broil for about two minutes on each side. Serve hot.

Holiday cooking

Tante Belle and Tante May, my great-aunts, used to claim that the time between Thanksgiving and Christmas just wasn't long enough to prepare for the holidays. After all, there were fruitcakes steeped with bourbon (or rum), pralines and candy, and cakes and pies that had to be prepared for the week-long celebration that lasted from Christmas to New Year's Day.

Everyone is busy in their respective kitchens, working from early morning until the sun goes down making all the goodies that are traditional fare for our large family. The aromas that emanate from the kitchen are absolutely divine!

I'm not much of a fruitcake fan, and although I do enjoy candy I'm not good at making it. What I am good at making is apple cake. This particular cake recipe comes from my Aunt Grace, otherwise known as Cina or Nanny, depending on which generation you're speaking with. She's in her nineties and has passed on many of her recipes to her nieces and nephews who, in turn, make them for her now.

On the Friday after Thanksgiving I always get a call from her.

"Celle, now don't forget to make some apple cakes for the holidays. You know how much everyone likes them," she murmurs in her soft voice.

What she's really telling me is that she expects at least one, perhaps two cakes, still warm from the oven, to be delivered to her personally during the holidays.

I get the hint and immediately begin cranking out apple cakes. They are moist, chock-full of apples, and they make great gifts – but be sure to stash a couple aside for your own family. They can be served warm or at room temperature. For a festive touch, spoon whipped cream on top of the slices and sprinkle with toasted pecans. They can be made a day or so ahead of time. Just be sure to wrap the cakes well in plastic wrap and then in aluminum foil to keep them moist and fresh.

Marcelle's Best Ever Apple Cake

Makes 1 large cake or 2 loaf cakes

2 cups of sugar
3 cups of all-purpose flour
3 cups of tart apples, peeled and chopped
1 teaspoon of baking soda
2 teaspoons of ground cinnamon
1 cup of chopped pecans or walnuts
1 teaspoon of salt
1¼ cups of vegetable oil
2 large eggs
2 teaspoons of pure vanilla extract

Preheat the oven to 350 degrees.

Combine the sugar, flour, apples, baking soda, cinnamon, nuts and salt in a large mixing bowl and mix well. Add the oil, eggs and vanilla, and stir to mix.

Spoon the mixture into a 9-inch tube pan, or divide the mixture into two equal portions and spoon it into two 9x5x3-inch loaf pans. Bake for one hour or until a toothpick inserted into the center of the cake comes out clean.

Remove the cakes from the oven and cool on a wire rack. Slide a thin knife around the edges of the cake and remove the cake from the pan. Let the cake cool completely before wrapping.

My other contributions to the holidays are roasted pecans and roasted garlic-flavored almonds. The pecans are a local favorite simply because pecans are so plentiful in south Louisiana. When the pecans start falling from the trees in the fall, people get out on their hands and knees and pick until their hands turn numb. Then the nuts are cracked and picked. The nuts can be stored in the freezer to be used throughout the year.

Remember my friend, Keith Courrégé? Well, he was the king of roasting pecans, and I offer you his recipe.

Basic Roasted Pecans

Makes 4 cups

4 cups of pecan halves
4 tablespoons of butter
1 tablespoon of salt

Preheat oven to 325 degrees.

Spread the pecans on a heavy baking pan and bake for 30 minutes.

Add the butter and stir well until all the pecans are coated. Bake for 15 minutes longer, sprinkle with salt, and stir well.

Bake for 15-20 minutes longer, and remove from the oven. Cool before storing in airtight containers.

I began roasting almonds several years ago when friends sent me a five-pound box as a gift. I didn't have any idea of what to do with so many almonds, so I began roasting them to give as gifts and to serve at holiday get-togethers. Make several batches of these roasted nuts and store them in airtight containers for up to three weeks.

I don't know about you, but I always cherish gifts from a friend's kitchen.

I have a little note someone gave me years ago when thanking me for her holiday treats.

It goes like this:

"Nothing represents the spirit of loving, nurturing and giving more than homemade gifts. They are made and given from the heart. They are something friends and family can make together."

That should give you some inspiration!

Roasted Garlic Almonds

1 tablespoon of unsalted butter
2 tablespoons of soy sauce
2 teaspoons of Tabasco
3 garlic cloves, mashed
1 pound of blanched whole almonds
3 teaspoons of Creole or Cajun seasoning of your choice
¼ teaspoon of dried red pepper flakes
Salt, to taste

Preheat the oven to 350 degrees.

Coat a rimmed baking sheet with the butter and sprinkle with the soy sauce, Tabasco and garlic. Scatter the almonds oven the sheet and stir with a fork until well coated. Sprinkle with 1½ teaspoons of the Creole or Cajun seasoning, dried pepper flakes and salt.

Bake for 10 minutes.

Sprinkle the almonds with the remaining 1½ teaspoons of Creole or Cajun seasoning and additional salt if desired. Stir with a fork and bake for 15 more minutes.

Cool the nuts before serving or storing in airtight containers.

The almonds may be stored for up to three months.

Holiday beverages

Rock, my husband, usually hates winter because of the shorter days and the rainy, cold weather. But once the north winds begin to blow, he gets into the swing of things. One year we had an uncommonly cold spell with temperatures dipping down into the 30s at night and not getting above 45 degrees for well over a week.

My tender tropical plants were stored in his workshop, where we hung several large spotlights to keep them warm. A roaring fire was built every evening when we came in from work, and we made pots of gumbo and soup to keep us warm.

One evening when we both claimed we had cabin fever, we invited several neighbors over to join us before the fire. Yet another pot of soup simmered on the stove, and I made a batch of hot apple cider.

While we sipped on the hot drink, talk turned to holiday beverages. Everyone agreed that eggnog is synonymous with the holidays. And although there are good commercial brands, I think there's nothing quite as good as homemade eggnog with beaten egg whites folded in right before serving.

Someone commented that hot coffee drinks are fun, and one neighbor said her favorite celebration beverage is a bubbly punch made with champagne. I recalled an old friend of the family who favored syllabub, a rich creamy drink that's ideal for holiday gatherings.

These days the food police warn us not to consume eggs that have not been cooked, so I cannot give you a recipe for eggnog made with raw egg yolks. So, do as I do: Buy a good-quality commercial brand and beat the egg whites (Always use fresh eggs from a reliable source.) until they hold soft peaks. Fold them into the eggnog and add bourbon or rum, to taste. Serve in cups and sprinkle with grated nutmeg and ground cinnamon. Yum! Oh, and you can serve it warm or chilled.

If you like bubbly, you'll like this punch!

Strawberry, Lime & Champagne Punch

Makes about 12 servings

1/3 cup of sugar
1 package (10 ounces) of frozen
    strawberries in syrup, thawed
1/2 cup of fresh lime juice
1/2 cup of brandy
1/2 cup of chilled club soda
2 bottles of chilled champagne
Strawberries and limes, thinly sliced
    for garnish

In a small saucepan, combine the sugar with one-half cup of water and simmer the mixture for five minutes, or until the sugar is dissolved. Let the sugar syrup cool completely.

In a food processor, puree the strawberries with their syrup and the lime juice and transfer the mixture to a large punch bowl by forcing the pureed berries through a sieve. Stir-in the sugar syrup and the brandy.

This mixture can now be stored in a covered container in the refrigerator for later use. When ready to serve, add chilled club soda and chilled champagne to the punch bowl. Garnish with strawberry and lime slices.

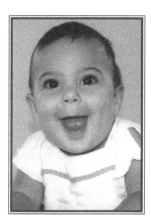

Typical of south Louisiana families, we have lots of great-nieces and great-nephews – and the number keeps on growing! Above is Olivia Domino, in 2006; at right is Eli Landry, roaming in my back yard in 2005.

Coffee lovers, this one's for you.

Mexican Coffee

Makes 5 cups

6 cups of water
½ cup of firmly packed light brown sugar
½ cup of regular-grind coffee
½ ounce of unsweetened chocolate
1 small tea bag of chamomile tea
1 tablespoon of ground cinnamon
2 whole cloves
½ teaspoon of pure vanilla extract

Combine the water and sugar in a heavy saucepan over medium heat and stir until the sugar dissolves.

Add the coffee, chocolate, tea, cinnamon and cloves, and bring to a boil. Reduce the heat and simmer, uncovered, for 15 minutes, stirring occasionally. Stir in the vanilla.

Strain through several thicknesses of cheesecloth. Serve hot.

And here's to Miss Camille, who loved syllabub. By the way, this is a thick, frothy drink or dessert that originated in England. I've often wondered how she came to like it so.

Syllabub

Makes 12 servings

¼ cup of sifted powdered sugar
½ cup plus 2 tablespoons of white wine
3 tablespoons plus 1 teaspoon of brandy
3 tablespoons plus 1 teaspoon of grated lemon rind
1½ tablespoons of fresh lemon juice
10 cups of heavy cream, whipped
Freshly grated nutmeg for garnish

Combine the sugar, wine, brandy, lemon rind and lemon juice in a large bowl. Beat until well-blended.

Fold in the whipped cream and spoon into serving glasses. Garnish with grated nutmeg.

On stuffings and dressings...

Before we head into the New Year, I have one last *bon mot* for you. Down here in the Deep South, we have dressings and we have stuffings, both of which sometimes confuse strangers, newcomers, or visitors, whom we refer to as being from "away."

Well, sometimes the vague distinctions disconcert even me. Let's see, dressings are usually, but not always, made with rice combined with meat or seafood, and, of course, a healthy dose of onions, bell peppers, celery and other seasonings. They can also be made with corn bread, day-old bread, or plain old crumbled saltine crackers.

These mixtures can be served as side dishes and are then referred to as "dressings," but they can also be used to stuff poultry (like turkey or other birds, and even, at times, fish) and sometimes vegetables like bell peppers, mirlitons or tomatoes – at which point the "dressing" becomes a "stuffing."

Over martinis one evening, a friend who was visiting from "away" asked me to explain this very subject.

Good old rice dressing made with ground chicken giblets, ground beef and pork, along with rice and lots of chopped green onions and parsley, is a must here in the South. It is served with baked or barbecued chicken and almost always at festive dinners. Corn bread dressing made moist with pan drippings from baked turkey and containing slightly crunchy bits of celery is *de rigueur* holiday fare.

Rock jumped into the conversation and said that although he likes both rice dressing and corn bread dressing each can be brought to new heights by adding plump, salty oysters to the mixture.

An old boyfriend of mine adored a rice, mushroom and water chestnut concoction with baked doves, baked ducks or fried quail.

Here is a recipe that combines corn bread, chicken livers, pork sausage, water chestnuts, and chopped spinach. It is also good with wild game, but it can certainly be served with poultry, beef or pork.

Naturally, this "dressing" can be stuffed into vegetables, thus transforming it into "stuffing."

Spinach & Corn Bread Dressing

Makes 8 to 10 servings

3 tablespoons of bacon drippings
  or vegetable oil
4 cloves of garlic, minced
1 bunch of green onions, chopped
1 cup of chopped celery
1 (10-ounce) bag of fresh spinach, cleaned,
  stemmed, and coarsely chopped
1 pound of chicken livers, chopped
1 pound of pork sausage, removed from
  the casing
4 cups of crumbled corn bread
Chicken broth
Salt and cayenne, to taste
2 small cans of sliced water chestnuts, drained
¾ cup of chopped fresh parsley leaves
½ cup of coarsely chopped pecans

Preheat the oven to 350 degrees.

Heat the bacon drippings or vegetable oil in a large saucepan over medium heat. Add the green onions, garlic, celery and spinach, and cook, stirring, until the vegetables are tender.

Add the livers and sausage and cook, stirring, until all pink in the meats disappears. Add the crumbled corn bread and enough broth to moisten the dressing. Season with salt and cayenne. Add the water chestnuts, parsley and pecans.

Pour into a baking dish and bake for about 45 minutes. Serve warm.

*Papa Rock and my great-nephew Shane Bennett sport
their outfits in our yard in the fall of 2004.*

No matter how crowded my calendar is during the holiday season, I always try to host a brunch for out-of-town visitors. As far as I'm concerned, brunches are quite civilized simply because the meal can be taken at leisure and there are no hard and fast rules about what can be served.

Personally, I like *grillades* – a Creole dish made with pieces of pounded veal or beef cooked in a delicious gravy – served over creamy baked cheese grits. Mama's menu of choice is sinfully rich biscuits accompanied with a cheese and egg casserole. My neighbor Jeri puts on the Ritz with her eggs poached in a cream and cheese mixture tinged with vermouth. When oysters are available, Rock does Eggs Benedict, but substitutes oysters for the Canadian bacon. Wow!

This casserole is just as popular as any of the aforementioned delicacies.

Brunch Casserole

Makes 10 to 12 servings

4 cups of cubed day-old French bread
2 cups of shredded cheddar cheese
10 large eggs, lightly beaten
1 quart of milk
1 teaspoon of dry mustard
1 teaspoon of salt
¼ teaspoon of cayenne
¼ teaspoon of onion powder
8 to 10 slices of bacon, cooked and crumbled
½ cup of sliced fresh mushrooms
½ cup of peeled, seeded, and chopped tomatoes

Generously butter a 9x13-inch baking dish. Arrange the bread in the baking dish and sprinkle with cheese.

In a bowl, combine the eggs, milk, mustard, salt, cayenne and onion powder.

Pour the mixture over the bread. Top with the bacon, mushrooms and tomatoes. Cover and chill up to 24 hours.

Preheat oven to 325 degrees. Bake uncovered for about an hour or until the mixture sets. Tent with foil if the top begins to overbrown. Serve hot.

Just when I think I can't stand another dreary, gray day, Nature blesses south Louisiana with a bright, clear day. Papa used to call it a "bluebird" day. Don't ask me why.

I head for the outdoors. The sunshine feels good on my face, and I get a surge of energy. The leaf-covered patio needs sweeping. I fluff up my beds of pansies and sneak over to my neighbor's yard to inspect her camellia bushes. Blossoms of pink, red and white nod in the breeze amid the faded brown landscape.

Above my head, the blue jays and redbirds dart among the stark, leafless cypress and oak trees.

On one such day, a neighbor walked down our lane bringing me a pot of bright red tulips, which further enhanced my good mood.

As I searched for just the right spot for my pot of tulips, the thought occurred to me that a colorful meal would be the perfect ending to a very pleasant day. I had several bright green artichokes, and there was some catfish and shrimp in the freezer. It would all be perfect for just such a meal.

First, the artichokes. I boiled a few to serve with a tart mayonnaise dipping sauce. The others were stuffed with crabmeat.

Boiled Artichokes

Makes 6 servings

3 artichokes, stems removed
  and leaves trimmed
6 cups of water
1 teaspoon of salt
1 teaspoon of freshly ground black pepper
½ teaspoon of dried oregano leaves
2 tablespoons of olive oil
1 teaspoon of granulated garlic

Rinse the artichokes in cool water. Place the artichokes in a large pot with the water and all of the remaining ingredients and bring to a boil. Reduce the heat to medium and cover the pot. Boil gently until the artichokes are tender, about an hour. Remove from the heat, drain, and cool.

Serve the artichokes with a mayonnaise sauce laced with a bit of lemon juice, black pepper and crushed garlic.

Artichokes Stuffed with Crabmeat

Makes 6 servings

6 artichokes
1 teaspoon of olive oil
1 teaspoon of salt
¼ teaspoon of white pepper
1½ pounds of lump crabmeat, picked over
  for shells and cartilage
Louis Sauce (Recipe follows)

Wash the artichokes in cool water and trim the stems and leaves.

Place the artichokes in a large pot and fill it half-full with water. Add olive oil, salt and white pepper. Bring the water to a boil, cover, and reduce the heat to simmer. Cook the artichokes until they are tender, about an hour. When a leaf pulls out easily, drain and cool the artichokes.

Remove the chokes from the centers of the artichokes. When you are ready to serve, fill the outer leaves and centers of the artichokes with crabmeat tossed in Louis Sauce.

LOUIS SAUCE
1 cup of mayonnaise
¼ teaspoon of Worcestershire sauce
¼ cup of minced green pepper
¼ cup of minced green onion
1 tablespoon of minced pimiento
Salt and black pepper, to taste
Hot sauce, to taste
1 tablespoon of fresh lemon juice

Combine all of the ingredients and chill.

The case for catfish

Some people turn up their noses at catfish thinking that they are nothing more than bottom-feeders with a muddy taste. But catfish caught in the great Atchafalaya Basin (not far from my abode) and farm-raised catfish are delicious. They're sweet and can stand up to a variety of preparations, including Catfish Creole, a favorite of my late father's.

Papa was an avid fisherman who spent a great deal of his leisure time in the Basin or on nearby Vermilion Bay. He was a happy man when he returned from his fishing trips with a mess of fresh fish. He had a fish-cleaning spot in the corner of the back yard equipped with a big slab of granite on a stand, a two-compartment sink with running water, and a big garbage can. There we gathered to watch him gut, scale and clean his catch. He was a surgeon with his knives, and he was also a good teacher who showed us all the parts of the innards and identified each fish as he cleaned it.

With a cold beer at his elbow, he

could stand for hours at this task.

When he was through with his chore, Mama gave the fish a final rinse while we all discussed how we were going to prepare "the loot," as Papa called it. On cue we would recite the litany – fried catfish, redfish *courtbouillion*, baked trout, stuffed snapper. One day he added to the list by creating this delightful catfish dish served over perfectly steamed white long-grain rice.

Catfish Creole

Makes 6 servings

6 catfish fillets (5 to 6 ounces each)
Salt and cayenne, to taste
4 tablespoons of butter
2 cups of chopped yellow onions
1 cup of chopped bell peppers
½ cup of chopped celery
1 (16-ounce) can of whole tomatoes, crushed
2 bay leaves
1 tablespoon of Worcestershire sauce
Tabasco, to taste
6 lemon slices
½ cup of minced fresh parsley leaves

Rub the fillets generously with salt and pepper.

In a large black iron skillet, heat the butter over medium heat. Add the onions, bell peppers and celery, and cook, stirring, until the vegetables are wilted, about five minutes. Add the tomatoes, bay leaves, Worcestershire sauce and Tabasco. Cook over a medium fire for 15 to 20 minutes, stirring occasionally.

Add the catfish fillets, cover the pot, and reduce the heat. Simmer for about 10 minutes, or until the fish flakes easily with a fork.

To serve, remove the fish with a spatula to serving plates and garnish with lemon slices and parsley. Spoon the sauce over steamed rice on the side.

Shrimp bisque is rich, creamy and sinfully good. Papa especially liked to enjoy this dish when we were at the camp on Vermilion Bay and he liked to tell the story about "the city-slicker" he took fishing a couple of times who showed him how to prepare this dish. Serve it with hot French bread and a cold, crisp, green salad. A chilled white wine washes it down nicely.

If you don't want the bisque as rich, decrease the amount of cream to one cup.

Shrimp Bisque

Makes 8 servings

2 pounds of medium-size shrimp
2 quarts of water
1 rib of celery, coarsely chopped
1 small onion, peeled and coarsely chopped, plus 1/2 cup of finely chopped onions
1 teaspoon of salt
½ teaspoon of cayenne
6 tablespoons of margarine
6 tablespoons of all-purpose flour
2 cups of heavy cream or half-and-half, slightly warmed
1 tablespoon of tomato paste
2 ounces of dry sherry

Peel and devein the shrimp and reserve the shells.

Place the shells in a stockpot with the water, the celery, the coarsely chopped onion, salt and cayenne. Bring to a boil and reduce the heat to low. Simmer for one hour. Remove from the heat and strain through a fine-mesh sieve. Measure six cups of stock and set aside.

In a heavy pot, combine the margarine and flour and, stirring constantly, make a medium-brown roux. Add the finely chopped onions and cook until wilted. Add the shrimp and cook, stirring, until they turn pink. Add the stock and simmer for 15 minutes. Turn off the heat and allow the mixture to cool for 15 minutes.

Pour the mixture into a food processor and process for 15 seconds.

When ready to serve, return the shrimp mixture to the pot and heat over low heat. Gradually add the cream or half-and-half and the tomato paste, blending well.

Add the sherry and simmer for 10 minutes or until the bisque thickens. Season with salt and cayenne if necessary. Serve warm.

Mardi Gras time!

Here in Louisiana we jump from the busy days of Christmas and New Year's right into the even more hectic season of Carnival, which begins on Twelfth Night.

Then it's several weeks, more or less, of balls, parades and various other parties to enjoy during the season. I like this time of year because my birthday is in February. In fact, I was a *Mardi Gras* baby, born on Fat Tuesday. Papa once said that I left the womb with beads around my neck and doubloons clutched tightly in my fat little hands.

There is no question that I have purple, green and gold blood coursing through my veins during this time of year as I await the celebration of both *Mardi Gras* and my birthday. No matter that these festive occasions have fallen on the same day only twice in my life so far.

Yes indeed, I get right into the spirit on Twelfth Night. I drag out all the *Mardi Gras* memorabilia I have accumulated through participation in balls, caught at parades and otherwise gathered, and I make various tableau throughout the house. The ring my king gave me the night I ruled as Cleopatra sits on a velveteen pillow alongside my headdress (Eat your heart out, Liz Taylor!), and various pieces of Mardi Gras jewelry, silver favors and special beads are given places of honor.

I urge and sometimes indeed insist that friends and family give me parties at any time during Carnival – and yes, even when my birthday falls after *Mardi Gras* day. One year my birthday fell on *Mardi Gras* eve and prior to that my friends duly honored me with all sorts of galas. It went along at a fast clip, when, alas, at dawn on my birthday I realized nothing, absolutely nothing, was planned for that evening. Everyone was going off to balls, parades and receptions. I realized that my favorite restaurants were either closed or packed to the gills with revelers.

Rock had just about had it with all the celebrating and suggested we stay home and have a quiet dinner for two.

That was fine with me (I was a little tired.) and we could enjoy dinner while listening to traditional New Orleans *Mardi Gras* tunes on the CD player.

Although I'm a great seafood lover, I'm equally fond of beef. I know, beef has gotten a bad rap these past few years, but I take my cue from my friend Julia Child who always advises "moderation in everything." Here was an occasion for my monthly indulgence.

Stuffed Filet Mignon

Makes 2 servings

5 tablespoons of olive oil
¼ cup of minced bell peppers
¼ cup of minced onions
¼ cup of cream cheese, seasoned with
    coarsely ground fresh black pepper,
    minced garlic, a pinch of dill, a few
    dashes of Tabasco, and a teaspoon
    of Creole mustard
2 filet mignons (about 8 ounces each)
1 tablespoon of soy sauce
½ teaspoon of coarsely ground black pepper

Heat two tablespoons of the olive oil in a skillet over medium heat. Add the bell peppers and onions and cook, stirring, until they are slightly wilted, about two minutes.

Combine the vegetables with the seasoned cream cheese and set aside.

Using a sharp knife, cut a pocket into the side of the filets about 2 inches long and 1½ inches deep, and stuff the steaks with the cream cheese mixture. Close and secure with toothpicks.

Rub the steaks well with a tablespoon of the olive oil, the soy sauce, and the black pepper. Heat the remaining two tablespoons of olive oil in a heavy skillet over medium-high heat. Cook the filets three to four minutes on each side depending on how you like your steaks – or you can grill them on an outdoor pit.

A salad of mixed greens and a perfectly baked potato finished out the menu, except for dessert, which instead of birthday cake was a batch of heavenly meringues topped with strawberries.

Meringues

Makes 6 servings

2 egg whites, at room temperature
Pinch of salt
½ teaspoon of cream of tarter
½ cup of sugar
½ teaspoon of pure vanilla extract
1 pint of strawberries, hulled, sliced, and
    sprinkled with a little sugar
Whipped cream

Preheat the oven to 225 degrees. Line a baking sheet with brown or parchment paper.

Beat the egg whites until frothy; add the salt and cream of tartar and continue beating until the egg whites form soft peaks. Add the sugar, a little at a time, beating in between the additions. After you have incorporated one-fourth cup of the sugar into the egg whites, add the vanilla. Continue to add the sugar. When all of the sugar has been added, beat two minutes longer at high speed until the meringue is stiff.

Drop the meringue into six mounds on the prepared baking sheet. Use the back of a metal spoon to shape the meringue, building up the sides to form shells or cups.

Bake until the meringues are lightly browned, about an hour. Turn the oven off and let the meringues stay in the oven for another 30 minutes or until cool.

With a thin-bladed knife, gently lift the meringues from the paper. Fill each shell with equal amounts of the strawberries. Top with whipped cream.

Index of Recipes
– Alphabetical –

Index of Recipes
– By Food Category –

Potatoes
Creamy Creamed Potatoes, 45
Escalloped Potatoes, 63
Potatoes Anna, 62
Potato Casserole, 63
Potatoes with Garlic and Cheese, 63

Poultry
Chicken & Oyster Pie, 84
Chicken Creole, 66
Chicken with Shallots & Artichokes, 67
Cobb Club Sandwich, 40
Keith's Baked Pecan Chicken, 69
Marinated Chicken with Thyme, 37
Rock's Barbecued Chicken, 53
Spinach & Corn Bread Dressing, 92
Sticky Chicken, 23

Preserves
Honey Pears, 35
Pickled Okra, 35

Rice
Baked Rice with Leeks, 73
Eggplant & Rice Dressing, 33
Rice with Caramelized Onions, 26

Roasted Garlic Almonds, 89

Salad
Chilled Beet Salad, 73
Tomato, Corn & Bean Salad with Tarragon, 37

Sauces
Creole Tartar Sauce, 15
Spaghetti Sauce with Olives, 29
Spaghetti Sauce with Bacon, 29

Shrimp
Grilled Shrimp with Smoked Sausage & Basil, 52
Marinated Grilled Shrimp, 46
Rock's Surf & Turf, 52
Shrimp & Crab Lafourche, 19
Shrimp Bisque, 96
Shrimp Casserole, 46
Shrimp Remoulade, 61
Skewered Shrimp with Zucchini, 40

Soup
Andouille & Black Bean Soup, 74
Cream of Leek Soup with Tasso, 71
Eggplant Soup, 74
Shrimp Bisque, 96
Sweet Red Bell Pepper Soup, 77

Stuffed Tomatoes, 42

Vegetables
Artichoke Bottoms with Lump Crabmeat, 19
Artichokes Stuffed with Crabmeat, 95
Boiled Artichokes, 95
Broiled Eggplant & Red Onion, 87
'Copper Pennies,' 22
Eggplant & Rice Dressing, 33
Eggplant & Veal Meatballs, 33
Jerusalem Artichoke Casserole, 82
Lima Bean Casserole, 82
Marcelle's Leeks & Tomatoes, 72
Marinated Vegetables with Basil, 37
Roasted Vidalia Onions, 20
Rock's Brussels Sprouts, 20
Skewered Shrimp with Zucchini, 40
Smothered Okra, 36
Spinach & Corn Bread Dressing, 92
Stuffed Banana Peppers, 77

About the Author

MARCELLE BIENVENU is a cookbook author and food writer who has been preparing Cajun and Creole dishes since the 1960s.

– Photography by Steve Comeaux, St. Martinville, Louisiana

A native of St. Martinville, Louisiana, in the heart of the Cajun country, she has written a weekly food column, "Creole Cooking," for *The Times Picayune* of New Orleans since 1984. She's worked as a researcher and consultant for Time-Life Books, contributing to a series of books titled *Foods of the World*. She's been featured in *Food & Wine, Southern Living, Redbook, The New York Times, Louisiana Life, Louisiana Cookin'* and *Acadiana Profile*.

She is the author of three books: *Who's Your Mama, Are You Catholic and Can You Make a Roux? (Book 1), Who's Your Mama... (Book 2)*, and *Cajun Cooking for Beginners*.

She co-authored several cookbooks with renowned chef Emeril Lagasse, including *Louisiana: Real & Rustic, Emeril's Creole Christmas, Emeril's TV Dinners* and *Every Day's A Party*. She also co-authored *Eula Mae's Cajun Kitchen* with Eula Mae Doré, a longtime cook for the McIlhenny family on Avery Island, and *Stir the Pot: The History of Cajun Cuisine*, with Carl A. Brasseaux and Ryan A. Brasseaux.

Ms. Bienvenu edited the 1987 edition of *The Times Picayune's Creole Cookbook*, originally published in 1901 and re-issued to celebrate the newspaper's 150th anniversary.

She owned and operated a restaurant, Chez Marcelle, near Lafayette, La., in the early 1980s, and has worked for several restaurants, including Commander's Palace and K-Paul's Louisiana Kitchen in New Orleans.

A graduate of the University of Southwestern Louisiana, she lives on Bayou Teche in St. Martinville, La., with her husband, Rock Lasserre.

Cookbooks by Acadian House Publishing

The Nation's leading publisher of authentic Cajun and Creole recipes

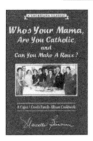

Who's Your Mama, Are You Catholic, and Can You Make A Roux? (Book 1)

A 160-page hardcover book containing more than 200 Cajun and Creole recipes, plus old photos and interesting stories about the author's growing up in the Cajun country of south Louisiana. Recipes include Pain Perdu, Couche Couche, Chicken Fricassée, Stuffed Mirliton, Shrimp Stew, Grillades, Red Beans & Rice, Shrimp Creole, Bouillabaisse, Pralines. (Author: Marcelle Bienvenu. ISBN 0-925417-55-6. Price: $22.95.)

Who's Your Mama, Are You Catholic, and Can You Make A Roux? (Book 2)

A 104-page hardcover book containing about 100 Cajun and Creole recipes, plus old photos and interesting stories about the author's growing up in the Cajun country of south Louisiana. Recipes include Shrimp Bisque, Andouille & Black Bean Soup, Crawfish-Okra Gumbo, Smothered Okra, Stuffed Tomatoes, Eggplant & Rice Dressing, Stuffed Pork Chops, Chicken & Oyster Pie, Apple Cake, Roasted Pecans. (Author: Marcelle Bienvenu. ISBN 0-9995884-6-X. Price: $19.95)

Cajun Cooking (Book 1)

...contains about 400 of the best Cajun recipes, like Jambalaya, Crawfish Pie, Filé Gumbo, Cochon de Lait, Chicken & Okra Gumbo, Sauce Piquante. Special features include a section on homemade baby foods and drawings of classic south Louisiana scenery. (ISBN: 0-9995884-9-4. Price: $22.95.)

Cajun Cooking (Book 2)

...picks up where Part 1 left off. It contains such delicious dishes as Shrimp & Crab Bisque, Fresh Vegetable Soup, Seafood-Stuffed Bellpepper, Broiled Seafood Platter, Yam-Pecan Cake. The recipes appear in the same easy-to-follow format as in Part 1, except they're in real large print for an arm's-length reading. (ISBN: 0-925417-05-X. Price: $15.95)

The Top 100 CAJUN Recipes Of All Time

...contains 100 recipes selected by the editors of *Acadiana Profile*, "The Magazine of the Cajun Country." For example, Boudin, Couche Couche, Maque Choux, Mirliton, Crawfish Etouffee, Chicken Fricassee, Pralines–the classics of South Louisiana cuisine. (Hardcover ISBN: 0-925417-52-1. Price: $16.95. Softcover ISBN: 0-925417-20-3. Price: $7.95)

The Top 100 NEW ORLEANS Recipes Of All Time

...contains 100 of the recipes that have helped to make New Orleans food world-famous. For example, Shrimp Creole, Red Beans & Rice, Blackened Redfish, Oyster Loaf, Muffaletta, Beignets, Café au Lait and King Cake. (Hardcover ISBN: 0-925417-51-3. Price: $16.95. Softcover ISBN: 0-925417-84-X. Price: $8.95)

Cajun Cooking For Beginners

A 48-page saddle-stitched soft cover book that teaches the basics of authentic Cajun cooking. It contains about 50 simple, easy-to-follow recipes; cooking tips and hints; a glossary of Cajun food terms, such as roux, gumbo, jambalaya and etouffee; and definitions of basic cooking terms, such as beat, blend, broil, sauté and simmer. (Author: Marcelle Bienvenu. ISBN: 0-925417-23-8. Price: $7.95)

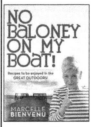

No Baloney On My Boat

This little 144-page cookbook is chock full of recipes for tasty and nutritious foods that can be enjoyed in the great outdoors. It's intended especially for fishers, hunters and campers who've been surviving on baloney sandwiches, sardines and Vienna sausage for far too long. The recipes can be prepared before leaving home, at the camp, in the beachhouse or on the boat (if it is equipped for cooking). (Author: Marcelle Bienvenu. ISBN: 0-925417-69-6. Price: $17.95)